Love & Fury

for Ellyn,
with affection. It was great to
meet you. Good luck with your
unfolding work.

love & fury

A Memoir

Richard Hoffman

BEACON PRESS, BOSTON

Beacon Press
Boston, Massachusetts
www.beacon.org

Beacon Press books
are published under the auspices of
the Unitarian Universalist Association of Congregations.

17 16 15 14   8 7 6 5 4 3 2 1

Excerpts from this book have appeared in
River Teeth: A Journal of Narrative Nonfiction and in the *Ocean State Review.*

This book is printed on acid-free paper that meets the uncoated paper
ANSI/NISO specifications for permanence as revised in 1992.

Text design by Yvonne Tsang
at Wilsted & Taylor Publishing Services

LIBRARY OF CONGRESS CATALOGING-IN-PUBLICATION DATA
Hoffman, Richard
Love and Fury : a memoir / Richard Hoffman.
pages cm
ISBN 978-0-8070-4471-1 (hardback) – ISBN 978-0-8070-4472-8 (ebook)
1. Hoffman, Richard, 1949—Family.
2. Authors, American—21st century—Biography. I. Title.
PS3608.O4785Z46 2014
813'.6–dc23
[B]   2013045470

IN MEMORY OF

Richard C. Hoffman Sr.

1925–2008

AND FOR

Kathi, Robert, Veronica,
Damion, and D

Every society is really governed by hidden laws,
by unspoken but profound assumptions on the
part of the people, and ours is no exception.
It is up to the American writer to find out
what these laws and assumptions are.
In a society much given to smashing taboos
without thereby managing to be liberated
from them, it will be no easy matter.

James Baldwin

Part One

The responsibility of a writer
is to excavate the experience of
the people who produced him.

JAMES BALDWIN

We're sitting in the kitchen, at the scarred Formica table, my father and my brother Joe and I, having just finished the kind of meal we have had innumerable times in the twenty-three years since my mother died: take-out hot dogs from "Yocco, the Hot Dog King" with a side of deep-fried pierogies, or maybe it was microwaved Lloyd's Roast Beef Barbecue from a plastic container in the fridge, or strip steaks on the George Foreman Grill, with a side of microwaved instant mashed potatoes. I can't recall for certain what we ate that night, maybe because my father has asked us to meet with him after supper to go over his will, and the two steel boxes have been there on the table next to the tall plastic bottle of orange soda throughout the meal, keeping their secrets to themselves. I know what's in at least one of them, though: birth certificates, death certificates, account numbers, records, directions, the deeds to graves. It's two weeks since he's been diagnosed with MDS, myelodysplastic syndrome, a condition that, at his age, eighty-one, almost always becomes leukemia. He has everything in order, he says. It's all right here in the boxes.

"Now the will's pretty simple," he tells us, "everything's split down the middle so there's nothing for the two of you to fight about." He has told each of us the same thing in the past two weeks, and Joe and I have talked about it on the phone. "You want the toaster oven or the Foreman grill?" my brother joked. It's true that there wasn't much to split up.

My father had a story he liked to tell about sitting down with my mother at the kitchen table once each month to pay bills and putting all the bills in my mother's stockpot and drawing them out one by one, writing checks till the money was gone. "And that was that," he'd say. "If we ran out of money before we got to you, well then you went back in the pot next month."

Once when I was young and knew, according to my father, neither the difference between shit and shine-ola, nor my ass from my elbow, on a holiday visit home from college, I chimed in with a lame coda to my father's anecdote, trying to augment the good humor of it, give it a little extra spin. As my father drew the story to its canonical close, "well then you went back in the pot next month," I wisecracked that I finally understood why we never had a pot to piss in, another expression of my father's. "You guys were using it as the Accounts Payable Department!"

My father looked at me blankly as if he didn't get it. Then, before I could compound my mistake by trying to explain it, he rose from his chair.

"You little punk," he muttered as he left the room.

I had tripped a switch and plunged my father from the safety of his lyric, humorous, emblematic scene into deep shame and remembered desperation, the very emotions that his ritual telling, with its shrug and goofball smile, its cavalier "fuck 'em" attitude, was meant to exorcise. I was of course the one who didn't get it, sitting there on my elbow with a shine-ola-eating grin on my face. I was not the one who had stood against a wall at six in the morning for the shape-up, hoping to get picked to work like a donkey for the next twelve hours. I was not the one who'd had to go down to the PP&L office with money made from cleaning out somebody's suburban garage just to get the lights turned back on. I was not the one who felt humiliated the year our Christmas presents came from the Salvation Army, complete with tags that said, *Boy, 6–8 years old.* My father had taken all those years and all that shame and locked them in a little box of a story, and just when he was clicking it shut again, as he had so many times before, I propped the lid open a moment longer with my fatuous cleverness, and a monstrous cloud, a genie of shame, escaped.

Everyone in my family considered themselves middle-class, all my aunts and uncles, each and every household, whether anyone had a job or not, regardless of what kind of work they did when there was work, regardless of whether or not they had "a pot to piss in."

We never used the word "class." My father called us working people. He always said we were working people, and he wanted me to be proud of it. I was a good student. School came easily to me, and I couldn't wait to be the first in my family to go to college. And my father, conflicted in ways that he showed by barking, shouting, kicking things, and occasionally knocking me down, let me know that he was scared for me, jealous, proud of me, and betrayed.

I remember the day I announced to my father that, football scholarship or not, I was going to college. "Whattya think, your last name's Rockefeller?" I had asked him for his signature on the loan papers I'd left on the kitchen table with the glossy view book from Fordham University. When I first brought home the booklet, with its views of a Gothic clock tower, stained-glass windows, a wrought-iron gate, my mother held it at arm's length and tucked her chin as if it smelled suspicious, but in fact she didn't have her glasses handy and held it that way because she was what she called "far-sighted."

"Classy-looking joint," she pronounced.

"We don't have that kind of money," my father said. "Look around here, knucklehead, you see a Cadillac out front? A swimming pool in the back?" I'm sure I said something insolent then because he was after me as I headed for the door. He grabbed the neck of my varsity jacket and we pushed and pulled and wrestled until I escaped, leaving him holding the jacket, inside out. As I turned in the doorway to shout something else and get a good hold to slam the door, I saw him turn it back right side out and, quietly, tenderly, brush it off and hang it in the hall closet. Later, when I came back, the papers were upstairs on my bed, signed.

My brother and I exchanged a look across the table. Neither of us is especially acquisitive. My brother has lived with my father in the house we grew up in for many years now; I've made my life elsewhere, and in our fifties neither of us was swinging at piñatas anymore. Besides, we both wanted to talk with him about his health, about how he was taking this news, and we wanted to assure him we'd be there for him through it all. He looked terribly pale and from time to time he would wipe his forehead with a ragged towel he kept next to him. Sweat beaded on his ashen face. Was it his illness that seemed to wring from him this sweat so strangely unaccompanied by warmth or color, or was it the fear, the grief, the agony he withheld from us seeping through his fatherly performance?

Sometimes I think I've had two fathers: the one who made me, and the one I've made of him. One I talked to on the phone, the other I talked to in my head. I was sitting there at the kitchen table, waiting for a moment when my brother or I might turn the conversation to how he was feeling, maybe tell him how we were feeling. On my way from Boston to Allentown, in the car, I'd been talking to him in my head.

I was listening to Greg Brown, Ted Hawkins, Coltrane's *A Love Supreme* on the way. Earlier, just about an hour after I left my house, he called my cell phone.

"Where are you?"

"I'm just entering Connecticut."

"Well, it's a blizzard here. We've got about three or four inches already."

"Really? Nothing here. Blue sky."

"Well, don't be fooled. There's no emergency here."

No emergency there. I'd been wanting to see him since he called to tell me of his diagnosis. After we hung up I had a conversation with him in my head in which we talked about dying. "We're old souls, you and I," I told him. "I don't know what happens, but I know that." I didn't really. I was looking for comfort in a suitably skeptical story. It was a thin jacket against the cold, but better than nothing. Besides, it would afford my father respect for whatever belief he held while not encouraging him to profess anything he didn't fully believe.

It was no doubt my need, not his, to have such a conversation. A writer, I'm always trying to say what eludes saying and always falling short. Or maybe it's my post-Catholic yearning for a metaphysics that makes this world a sad Platonic derivative of a better one. In truth, I can't bring myself to profess anything wholeheartedly; it's all made of words, I tell myself, and as a writer I know well what quicksilver words can be. Or maybe this is what children of any age need from their parents: *where will you be when you're no longer with me?*

It was my mother who believed in the afterlife. "We'll all be together again one day," she would say and waggle her index finger back and forth to squelch dissent. "Nobody can say it's not true." My father seemed, sometimes, to expect that she was waiting for him. Other times he would speculate about things metaphysical, but that often ended in a wisecrack or a shrug. It was as if he acknowledged beforehand that certain things were unknowable, that you could not draw conclusions, only doodle in the margins. Some years ago, during one of my flirtations with Buddhism, I'd left the magazine *Tricycle* on a chair in the living room, and when I returned he was thumbing through it. "Where'd you get this?"

I told him I was intrigued with Buddhism because it was more a philosophy than a religion, and that I liked it that there was no God, only a path to try to stay on. I probably said a few other hokey things in a zeal that's since cooled, but my father asked me what I thought about reincarnation. He said he'd watched a monk on TV discuss it, that the guy said that you get to keep trying to get to heaven, that there's no such thing as hell, and that it takes most people several lifetimes; if you don't make it this lifetime, then you come back and try again. "Is that a Buddhist idea?"

I said that it seemed so to me. "Well, that makes sense," he said. "No wonder the world's such a mess. All the good people keep leaving."

Soon after my mother died, he retired, at age sixty-four, and for the next twenty years he hardly left his recliner by the window. My brother and I both worried he was depressed. He seemed fine as long as his sixty-inch rear-projection television was on (and loud; you could hear it half a block up the street), and it was nearly always on: sports channels, mostly, but also cop dramas, movies, and when he was alone, porn.

Joe and I wanted to get him help with whatever continued to afflict him, depression or post-traumatic stress, to either of which, it seemed to us, he held clear title. Once he told me that sometimes during the day he sat there in his chair just thinking, and that when he looked up at the clock, hours had passed. "What if you had all your thoughts at once," he asked me, "do you think that would be heaven or hell?"

In our household, it's my daughter Veronica who's most given to spiritual questions. A few years ago, she prodded me about my atheism, about my turn, long before she was born, from Catholicism, from religion in general. "So, Dad, you really think that when you die that's it. That there's nothing after that?"

"Well, think about it. There is no 'after that,' not for the person who's dead."

"But what happens to you?"

"I think you just become part of the fabric of things. You get buried or burned, and everything gets used making new life. That seems beautiful to me, don't you think?" I may have used the Buddhist metaphor of a raindrop falling into the ocean. I may have quoted the Canadian poet Irving Layton: "Death is the name of beauty not in use."

"But that's your body, Dad. I'm not talking about your body. I'm talking about *you*."

"Yes, but I don't think there's a me separate from my body. I think I'm a story, maybe a poem, that my brain composes. That's how come I've been so different at different times in my life. I'm composing from the materials at hand to be what I need to be. Once I don't need to be anything, I can let all that go. I mean, it will go when my brain dies."

"No, wait. You said *you* were composing yourself, not your brain. Your brain is what you use to do it. What about *that* you? See what I mean?"

"I just think that all that makes me useful or important is what I do, and this one life is all the time I have to do it in. Maybe you live on in other peoples' memories."

"Aarrrrgghhh! You are so frustrating!"

I didn't mean to be. It just seems to me that to believe in a separate spiritual destiny is a kind of metaphysical flight from our common predicament: we're dying. And what is perhaps worse: people we love die. But I understand her yearning, and her wonder. It is impossible not to wonder what happens to the dead. To insist that nothing at all happens is one thing, but not to *wonder* means refusing to allow the play of imagination on the very ground that probably gave rise to it. Whatever else might our inescapable fear be for, if not for us to transform it to wonder? It is foolish to put all of one's energy into not speculating, into a refusal to allow the mind both comfort and enchantment. Why diminish life? In this case the absence of dogma is the same as dogma; both positions are orthodoxies that forbid the myriad stories that offer themselves: not for belief, but for further wonder. It is to answer *What if?* with *So what.*

"It's a death sentence is what it is. Clear and simple." I'd been on the phone with him from my desk where in the ten minutes since he told me of his diagnosis, I was Googling and scrolling through websites about myelodysplasia, cherry-picking any stray bit of information that made things more hopeful. A premalignant condition. Often leads to leukemia. Often isn't always. "What kind of treatment are they talking about?"

"It's all about good days now. So long as there are some more good days I'll hang in there and fight. Once there are no more good days ahead, then the hell with it."

"I'm looking at it on the Internet right now. Some people beat this thing."

"Not when you're eighty. Don't be fooled. When you're eighty, you don't beat anything." There was no self-pity in his voice. There was something to his inflection, his timing, his timbre, that was different, something that seemed strange and out of place to me. I figured he was in some kind of shock.

"I want to read up about this and talk to some people here," I said. "I'll call you tomorrow."

"You do that."

Half an hour later, my brother called me. "Yeah, hi," he said. "Dad told me to call you. He said call your brother and see if he's okay. He said you seem to be taking this worse than he is."

Soon after that I had a dream: I was in a room with a giant map of the world on the wall. I held a long wooden pointer with a black rubber tip like the nuns used to use in school. My father was sitting on a kind of black leather throne with a gold seal of some sort above it while I advised him, explaining that this little war here, and this one here, and this one, and this one, were threatening to soon run together and become World War III. As I waited for his response, I saw fire at the windows, fire all around outside. It had begun. "I told you! I warned you!" I yelled at him.

"Yes, but what the hell did you expect me to do about it?"

How do people know how to grow old, how to cope with diminished physical prowess, with pain and stiffness, how to "act their age?" My Aunt Kitty, even at her ninetieth birthday party, insisted, "Don't you treat me like an old lady! I'm not an old lady!" And we had only her chronological age as evidence; nothing else, nothing in her behavior anyway, suggested she was wrong. At her party she wore a golden plastic tiara one of her great-grandchildren had bought for her, several leis around her neck, jingling bracelets, and high heels. Though the party was in her honor, she went from table to table making sure people were having a good time, sometimes chiding the shy, pulling them from their folding chairs and leading them across the room to introduce them to someone. The party took place at an assisted-living facility where my aunt volunteered. She lived alone in her own home and drove to the facility every day "to help take care of the old people."

I recall watching my aunt at that party and thinking that if her joie de vivre was denial, then I hoped I had developed something like her capacity for it.

Only a year after that party, she fell in her living room with her well-dusted Hummels and dolls and family photos covering every surface, and broke her ankle. She was able to turn on her television for company, but she couldn't reach the telephone. One of her five daughters found her that evening when, unable to reach her by phone, she grew alarmed.

When Margaret, no young woman herself, couldn't get her off the floor, she said she was going to call for an ambulance. "The hell you are! You just bring me some ice for this thing. I'm just going to stay put and get better."

"Mother, I can't even get you off the floor, and the bathroom's upstairs."

"You just bring me some ice cubes in a tea towel for this here ankle, and a coffee can to piss in. I'll be all right."

Although my aunt was treated at the hospital and sent back home, things were never the same. Her daughters took turns taking care of her in their homes, after bringing her back to her own little house of knickknacks and porcelain dolls and framed photographs for a few hours a day just so she could be there, just to try to help her hold on to her life.

As she wasted, she lost her hearing and would not even consider a hearing aid. We experienced her as withdrawing, and my father, in our telephone conversations, always referred to her as "fading" or "disappearing."

I remember, sometime after that, sitting in her living room with my father, who teased her, loudly, "Jesus, Kitty, you're disappearing. There ain't nothing to you no more. You were always a big strapping girl!"

"Ha," she said, "I was never big, don't you dare call me big." And she turned to me and winked, "I had a pretty nice shape on me, though; a pretty nice shape!"

My father, on the other hand, began referring to himself as old soon after my mother died. He was fifty-nine. If Joe or I tried to convince him to take a trip—in my case to come to visit his grandchildren in Boston—or even to just get out and have some fun, he'd reply, "Leave me alone. I'm an old man and I just want to sit here on my ass."

And in the long view that's what he did for nearly a quarter century after my mother's death. But that's too dismissive. And although he was clearly depressed, I don't want to reduce him to a diagnosis. For company, he had his huge TV, and if he was awake it was on. (Actually, I came into the house on more than one occasion to find him asleep in front of it, even though I could hear it a block away when I parked the car.) Staying in the house, especially visiting with kids, was hard. There was no escape from the massive, booming presence of that TV; it vibrated the walls, the floors. If you went upstairs to bed, you lay there until the late show and then the late-late show were over.

&

It was a gray November day in 2006 and I was in the supermarket when my cell rang, by the dairy case if I remember correctly. I saw the call was from "HOME" and figured it was Veronica, maybe asking me to pick something up.

"Daddy, are you coming home soon?"

"Soon as I check out here. I'm at the supermarket. Why?"

"I need to talk to you."

"Why? What's up?" I was keeping my tone light, but only because I could hear panic edging into her voice.

"Just come home."

"Why? What's happened? Veronica?"

"Daddy, just come home."

I rushed around the store, shopping list in hand, worry mounting. Veronica was only eighteen, but she was already a junior at Boston College, studying nursing. Had she failed a test? Had she cracked up her car?

"Sit down," she said when I had piled the groceries onto the kitchen table and taken off my jacket. She handed me some kind of stick, something like a thermometer with a window in it. In the window were two pink stripes. Although I'd never seen one of these before, I knew what it could only be. In the chair across from me, her legs pulled up so that her chin was on her knees, Veronica looked terrified.

"Well, wait a second," I said, "one of these lines is pretty faint, and it doesn't really extend as far as the other. Besides . . ."

"Dad."

"I know. I know. I'm just trying to slow things down so I can take this in."

"But what should I do?"

I can't recall exactly how the conversation unfolded. She

did tell me how it happened, how she and a guy she knew from high school had met again at a party and gotten carried away. "It was only one time!" she blurted.

I made a face at her.

Laughter through tears. "But what do I do now?"

"It all depends what you want to do."

"Mom's going to tell me to get an abortion."

The way she spoke the word "abortion" spoke volumes. The thought crossed my mind that she might carry this baby to spite her mother and her mother's feminism, which of course had afforded her the choice, among so many other things in her life, in the first place. This was quickly followed by the thought, the understanding really, that for all her demonstrated competence in the world and her quick intellect, she was still an adolescent daughter struggling to become autonomous, and that realization made this whole situation seem even sadder.

"It's your decision to make."

"What do you think?"

What I thought—or at least thought I thought—was that this was not the time in her life for a baby, and not with a young man she hardly knew (and whom I'd never met!). If she wanted to have a child with him, she could choose to do that—later. This was an accident, a mistake, and an ill-timed invitation to a new and very different life, an invitation to be declined.

But what I felt, and what seemed to easily overwhelm my thinking, was something else entirely. I felt a hot splash of joy right in the center of my chest.

&

My father is explaining that he thought it best to name my brother as executor of the will, since he is local. He has also given him power of attorney when it comes to medical decisions. Well, he hasn't actually filled out the paperwork, including a Do Not Resuscitate order, but he assures us he is going to do so. His signature there will ratify something he'd said to me on the phone a week or so earlier. "Just promise me that when I go you don't let them bring me back, you hear? For Christ's sake, it's bad enough to have to die once." I know he's had a similar conversation with my brother, so there's something about this meeting at the scarred and wobbly table that is formal, official, like closing on a house. My father is "passing papers." Earlier he'd said, "After supper tonight I'd like to sit down with my sons and go over some things," as if we were not the sons he was referring to. And in fact there is something detached and ceremonious about the way this is unfolding. "So. Any questions before I close up this box? Anything unclear you want me to go over again? No? Good."

Then, the silence uncomfortable, I start to gather the remaining dishes, rise to take them to the sink. "Sit. Sit," he says. "There is something else. Something else I want to talk to you boys about." Joe and I sneak a look at each other: you boys?

But whatever my father had planned to say, or at least the words he'd planned to use, won't come; tears, which he stanches with difficulty, arrive in their stead. "I'm sorry," he says, "I made a mistake once, a big mistake, and I don't want it to cause any more trouble. Joe, I think you know a guy named Beerman. I think you went to school with him." My brother is nodding, his brows knit, wondering what's coming. "Well, his aunt is a woman named Amanda Schuler. I don't know if that name means anything to you."

It does. To me. And I can see my brother knows where this is going, too.

I can remember my father slamming the door on his way out to visit her. He and my mother had been arguing. It was right before Christmas, either the first or second since our move to this house, so I would have been fourteen or fifteen. I've never considered this before, but thinking back to my father in a coat and tie—something he never wore—groomed and cologned on his way out the door to his girlfriend's house, farther west than our house on Thirteenth Street, farther into the wealth of the city, my father was, perhaps, trying desperately for the bourgeois life denied him in the semi-squalor of our family. There was not only the heartbreak of my two brothers wasting away in their wheelchairs, doomed by Duchenne muscular dystrophy, not to mention their constant need for care, but also my mother's less-than-respectable family—Helen, Cory, Etta, and Kenny: without education, alcoholic, vulgar, poor. My father's prospects had just improved: he was hired as recreation director for the city. For years he had worked as a coach at the Boys Club, as a laborer, then as a city health inspector, all the while umpiring and refereeing for extra cash and his love of sports. Now he was finally getting to do what he loved. I imagine it felt as if a new life were possible.

"Well, you might someday hear from this guy Beerman that your dad had an affair with his aunt, so I wanted you to know that it's true. I'm not proud of the fact. I was selfish and weak and I know I hurt your mother terribly. But I just wanted you to know so you don't someday get in a brawl or something with this Beerman kid trying to deny it." The look on my brother's face, my fifty-four-year-old brother who I don't believe has ever been in a fistfight in his life, is perplexed. When my father turns his head to talk to me, Joe allows himself an amused shake of the head.

"And Dick, the worst thing is that I let you down." I was

ready to protest, but the hand came up in the STOP sign. "You were dealing with a lot back then, and I wasn't there for you. You needed your dad, and I wasn't there for you." He was biting his lower lip, eyes welling again. "I'm sorry. I want to apologize to both of you boys."

Some fifteen years earlier I had told him about being raped by my Little League coach—what he meant by "dealing with a lot back then." I had written about it in a memoir that sent that coach, who was still violating young boys, to prison. My father had been instrumental in putting the book in the hands of people who knew where the coach was. He took it on himself as a moral failing he had to put right, and I'd considered the account more than squared.

While my father was with Amanda, I'd stayed home in the evenings, watching TV with my brothers, helping my mother care for them, and sometimes trying to console her as she wept and raged at my father.

"And I imagine, I don't know, but I imagine that it's good for you to know that your mother and I got through that okay. She took me back. She forgave me. And we were in a real good period in our life together when she got sick. That's the hell of it." He took a moment to steady himself. "But I want to apologize to you two boys."

I remember thinking that yes, it was the boys to whom he wanted to apologize.

I waited until I was sure he was finished, not wanting to risk the hand again. I recounted the enormous pressures he faced, day after day, caring for two sick and dying children, the financial pressures, the emotional pressure, the knowledge that there was only one end to the story. I said I didn't blame him.

"Aw, you're just trying to let me off the hook. You don't need to do that. I don't want you to do that. Not just-like-that"—he snapped his fingers—"I don't want you making excuses for me."

He was right. As I was speaking it had occurred to me that my mother had been under all those pressures, too, had felt that despair, that terrible doomed love for her hopeless children, and had had to feel his rejection and betrayal besides. I am also my mother's son.

I remember her leaning on the sink, weeping over a stack of dirty dishes. I'd seen her from behind and her posture drew me to her. I placed a hand on her shoulder and she went on crying. Behind us, in the next room, my brothers were watching TV: Bobby, fifteen, in his wheelchair; Joey, eleven, hugging his knees on the floor; Mikey, nine, in the wheelchair that used to be Bobby's. "What am I going to do?" my mother sobbed. "What am I going to do?"

Before my brother Bobby grew weak, falling down, unable to get up, before he was diagnosed with Duchenne, and before my brother Joe was born, and then Mike, who never walked, my mother was a singer. She sang the whole day long: *Shine little glow worm, glimmer glimmer. Bewitched, bothered, and bewildered. Don't sit under the apple tree with anybody else but me.*

My mother sang in clubs during World War II. My aunt told me this is how my parents met. Of course, I always imagined it Hollywood-style: my mother at the microphone, spotlit in a sequined dress, a band behind her in the semidarkness, singing some torch song while my father, looking handsome in his dress uniform, medals above his heart, his tie knotted just so (as he had tried to show me time and again before finally giving up and buying me a clip-on), listened appreciatively from a small table across the smoky room. Mood indigo.

But recently my father told me the story a little differently. Oh, I'd already long since understood that my version was fantasy. My mother in a slinky sequined dress? Please. And my father was a private back from basic training, awaiting orders. And a "club," in Allentown, is a bar room, dark, with usually only a diamond-shaped, face-sized window in the door and a few frosted glass bricks to let in some light. A couple of years ago I asked him about it and he smirked and waved his hand in that way of his that means "Bah." Or "Go on," a kind of erasure to make room for what he would say.

"It was up at the VFW, and your mother was in there with her mother and Kenny, her stepfather. Kenny was a blowhard when he was drunk, a loudmouth. He was a regular and had a kind of gang there. Him and Etta were up there all the time. And that night he was on his feet and telling everybody to pipe down, pipe down, his daughter was going to sing. Your mother didn't want to. She asked him to stop. 'My daughter Dolly's going to sing a song!' he kept saying, and I believe if she hadn't got up to sing it would have got ugly. So she did. She was a little shy but she had a great voice. You know your mother could always sing. And I don't remember if I asked her out that night or called her later." I asked him if he remembered what she sang that night and he said he didn't.

Her songs, her singing, hung on for a while, though not for long. I remember my mother singing and ironing:

> (clump) Come onna my house, my-eye house,
> I'm gonna give you ca-an-dy. (clump)
> Come onna my house, my (clump) house,
> I'll make you feel (clump) da-an-dy.

Come onna my house: My mother is stirring soup made from boiling half a dozen franks in salt water, two or three potatoes and half an onion cut up in it, with parsley and a dash of pepper. Supper after supper of this. Supper is our word. We eat supper. "They" have dinner. Out in the "west end" of town, where "the Rockefellers" live, they have dinner.

Or "hamburger soup": meat boiled till it is gray, floating in the water it's been cooked in, not skimmed, lenses of slick fat floating and rainbowing the florescent kitchen light, two or three potatoes and half an onion cut up in it, with parsley and a dash of pepper. Supper.

On Mondays (also the day my mother did laundry and hung it, billowing, on clotheslines the length of the yard) we had a supper called "cream-dry beef." And every Monday my father would explain, again, that this creamed and dried beef was also called "shit on a shingle," the shingle being the slice of toast over which the salty thick goop was ladled. I loved it because it was army food. I loved it like my father's paratrooper regalia, and his bayonet in its sheath. I used to look at the stains on that blade, wondering if they were blood, if my father had killed Nazis with it. I only ever saw my father use the bayonet to open old paint cans that had crusted shut; eventually the tip snapped off of it, and it became even more useful for that task. I had the chance, recently, to order it—Creamed Dried Beef—in a southern diner, and although they plopped it on a biscuit and garnished it with a sprig of parsley, it still tasted good to me. Whether I acquired a taste for it via my father's emphatic belly-patting pronouncements each week, "Man, that's good!" or would have found it tasty anyway, I can't say. So much of my life is history, I don't know if anything, any soul or essence or self preceded it. I'll leave that to the geneticists, since by the time I became aware of myself as someone distinct from the person my parents believed they were speaking to, by the time, that is, that I had enough inside to try to manipulate the outside, I was already brimful with history.

Home from the store, my mother divides up the S&H Green Stamps between Bobby and me so we can paste them in their squares in the redemption booklet. For five thousand points you can get a nice set of tea towels. For ten thousand a set of cups and saucers. Fifty thousand will get us a floor lamp that would "go nice" in the living room.

Que sera, sera, my mother sings, *Whatever will be, will be. The future's not ours to see. Que sera, sera.*

"Your mother and I got through that okay. She took me back. She forgave me."

What else could she do? What choice did she have? I wonder sometimes what choices she ever had. My mother grew up in rural poverty during the Depression, illegitimate, with a drunken stepfather and three younger sisters, and school ended after eighth grade. And yet she sang. What love—is there another word for it? Courage? Generosity?—to have been kept from ever opening the gift, but to pass it along to her children just the same and not demean it or throw it away in frustration. What wisdom, astonishing in its offhandedness, to have passed along also the wish to open it, the yearning to be able to one day open it, the longing to live beyond mere duty and endurance.

My father would most likely have encountered the word *patriarchy* as a ten-letter gap in one of the crossword puzzles he did with a pencil sharpened with a knife so the lead had a sculpted quality, rounded at the tip and smooth, not pointy, so it wouldn't tear the soft paper, and so it wouldn't incise the letters onto the page, which would make them harder to erase. Erasing, correcting, changing your mind when you were wrong, was a given; in fact, if you didn't have to do this at least several times to complete the puzzle, it was too easy. That's why each of his whittled pencils was capped with a pink wedge of eraser, soft rubber that didn't wear away the surface of the page, that gave you as many chances as you needed.

No one outside a marriage can really know its features: its ecstasies and regrets, its disappointments, reassurances, tendernesses, cruelties, secrets, truces, promises, compromises, least of all a child of that marriage. I can only say how it seemed to me; when I was young, before the future became a source of dread and inevitable grief, my parents were happy. They were in love: I recall enough of their touching and joking and kissing and flirting back when Bobby and I were young to feel sure of this. And I believe that "in love" or not, they loved each other continuously, even when their angers burned hot as hatred.

This will not come clear. It can't. There is no binary good/bad, glad/sad conclusion to be reached. When I have spoken of my family in the past, there is always someone who wants to know how such love and fury could coexist, and I don't understand the question. It seems either naive or disingenuous. Families seem to me to be *made* of love and fury. The world is mostly water; we are mostly water; life itself is mostly water, but we don't ask how such hydrogen and oxygen can coexist. We just drink it and live. Maybe we wish it were champagne, or root beer, or cider, but we're not foolish enough to wish it were liquid hydrogen, or liquid oxygen.

When my mother was dying, my father proposed to her again. My aunt Marie told me this coming from my mother's room where she lay struggling for breath. My aunt blew her nose in a tissue and smiled through tears: "Your mother said yes." I have no business dismissing that as sentimentality, nor is it any of my business what either of my parents said. And yet, if my mother had had no choice years earlier, she certainly didn't have one then. And there is always, intrusively and insistently, the thought that she had in fact already made her choice, moving smoke by smoke, pack by pack of Chesterfields, toward the only escape available to her. And even if she were still hurt and angry, wounded and furious, she could not have refused my father the consolation he was seeking; she didn't have it in her.

And neither do I. I am also my mother's son.

"It's a great relief," my father says, rising from the table and reaching for his footed aluminum cane, "a great relief to me to get that off my chest." The meeting is over. Joe and I sit there at the table and watch him make his way slowly into the living room to his recliner. He reaches for the remote and in a moment the TV comes on, loud enough to feel it through the floor.

I have a memory of a particular evening that has been with me so long it's become a little story. I would have been about six, I believe, having just started school. I think that's right because closely associated with this memory is the image of a flat, sheet-metal mannequin of a traffic cop that was rolled on its round base into the middle of the crosswalk outside St. Francis of Assisi School. Janus-like, he was painted on both sides with a whistle in his mouth and a white-gloved hand raised in the gesture STOP. Just after the final bell in the morning, two eighth-grade boys would fetch him and roll him back to the curb until the afternoon. But it is my father's hand I recall, abruptly raised in that gesture: STOP.

Bedtime was ritualized, a snack of little saltine peanut-butter sandwiches washed down with milk under my mother's supervision, my brother Bobby and I poking and stalling, never tired, never ready for bed, and brushing our teeth at the kitchen sink before we ran into the living room to say good night to our father.

I can't remember whether Bobby ran ahead of me to kiss our father good night or if I was first. My mother isn't part of this memory, either. In the little story, self-enclosed and still radiating bewilderment more than half a century later, I ran into the room as always to kiss my father's rough and stubbled cheek and say, "I love you. Good night, Daddy!" the words themselves a ritual, when suddenly his hand comes up: STOP. I can still see that hand, big as my whole face, in the timeless moment before it shifts and invites, requires, a handshake instead of a kiss, a quick pump up and down and a little squeeze before letting go. "Good night, son."

The memory ends there; everything else is outside its frame. I don't understand. I'm stunned by this break in the routine and by something more that I have not fully plumbed even now, a father and grandfather, a son orphaned in my sixtieth year.

My father cursed at just about everything he couldn't get to do his will: nails he couldn't pull with a claw hammer, screws and nuts too small for his fingers, lugnuts the garage had tightened with an air gun, all were "this fuckin' thing!" Goddamnits abounded. An occasional "cocksucker" for emphasis. There was nothing cool about my father, a man of many exasperations with a vocabulary to match. He wanted life to be otherwise, but he knew full well that life would never change. I suspect he wished that he were different, better, gentler; he seemed to blame himself for being the man he was: suffering, shattered, at a loss, and insufficient.

If I were to portray my father solely as a man who struggled to stretch the few dollars he could make in order to meet his family's needs, that would be a true, as well as familiar, story told in tribute to a steadfast and quietly heroic man. But if I also include his parallel struggle, to stretch the few inadequate ideas he was given, as a working man, with which to meet his family's needs for love, meaning, and justice, it is less comfortable, but no less true, no less crucial to an accurate portrayal of his life.

My brothers' illnesses, their hopelessness and progressive debilitation, required some metaphysical context; if not an explanation, then significance at least, and I think the Catholic focus—at least in those days—on the redemptive nature of suffering, may be the key to understanding my parents' inner life. My mother's conversion, at first mere convenience, allowing my parents to marry at Sacred Heart Church, no doubt became deeper and more real as life dealt the cards, the unholy cards, one by one, and mercilessly. It seems proof, at least to me, of the utility of her faith, its assistance in keeping some kind of hope alive in order to get through the days. Her faith, however, the practice of it, anyway, died with my brothers. It was no longer necessary. The same was true for my father, who had had a lifetime of Catholic understandings to slough.

Not long before he died, we were sitting in the living room talking about my mother. I said that I thought she had always felt guilty despite herself because the muscular dystrophy that killed my brothers is a genetic disease that travels in the maternal bloodline. My father was silent for a long time. Sometimes in our conversations he would fall silent like this. I'd come to expect and accommodate it. If I pressed on he might become agitated. Sometimes he would fall asleep, his chin on his chest, somewhere midway in the conversation. Other times he would bite his lower lip, a thoughtful glower on his features, then point the remote and turn on the TV. So I stood and went into the kitchen for a snack.

When I returned a few minutes later, I could see he was struggling, unsuccessfully, to hide his tears. "You know for a long time I believed it was my fault. It was punishment." I wanted to ask for what, but that's not how our give-and-take ever went; if he was going to tell me, he would. So I said it wasn't anybody's fault. "I don't believe it anymore. Not really. I don't really believe it. But they always said it was a mortal sin. So I believed I must have done something to damage my sperm. I jerked off too much. When I was a kid. And when I was in the army. My seed was no good. It was punishment."

It was hard to know how to react to his tears because I didn't know if he was feeling punished still, or if he was crying for himself for having ever been oppressed by such absurdity. I sat there with my bag of chips and can of soda, attending him.

"Still, you can't help it," my father said, his thumb and forefinger wiping tears from both eyes. "You feel responsible. You're the parent. You can't help it."

&

It's January 2007 and I'm in bed with pneumonia. Or maybe it was a back injury I sustained stupidly shoveling snow after weeks in bed with pneumonia. There was a knock at the bedroom door, and I looked up from my reading at a tall, handsome young man, Jamaican, black, with dreadlocks and a gentle but frightened look on his face. Although I already knew who he was, had been told he was coming, he introduced himself: Damion Smith. I beckoned him in, shook his hand, and gestured for him to sit at the foot of the bed, the only place available. I propped myself up on my pillows and tried to convey a sense of ease I wasn't feeling. I admired him. It took courage for a twenty-four-year-old black man to place himself in this scene. I don't recall precisely how the conversation unfolded, but he told me that he wanted me to know that he wasn't going to run away, that he wanted to do the right thing. (Later, I'd find out that several members of his family wanted to spirit him back to Jamaica, afraid that "that white girl's father" would kill him.)

I asked questions to try to get to know him and put him at ease. He told me about growing up in Jamaica with his father's family and being sent here to live with his mother when he was thirteen. I found out he wanted to write songs—hip-hop, reggae—and perform. We talked about how important it is to have an art in your life, an art that sustains you, that you continually work to perfect, no matter what else you have to do to get by. I probably defaulted to the professor talking to one of his students with the intention of being encouraging. "That's how you keep your soul alive," I said. I wince when I think of that now, my bedridden Polonius act.

At the same time, it was impossible not to grasp the clichéd nature of the situation: young man meeting his beloved's father, hoping for his blessing (though not exactly asking for her hand—absurdly late for that!). That may even be why the conversation ranged so far, touching upon his music, my writing, basketball, food. It's amazing to think back on it: I can only conclude we were terrified of each other.

Resisting the script seems also to have meant refusing to ask certain questions, like "Do you have a job? How exactly do you see yourself involved? Have you and Veronica talked about marriage?" (I certainly hoped not. They barely knew each other. There would be a time for that if their hearts took them there.)

On the immediate question of whether Veronica should go on and have the baby, Damion was clear: "I don't go for that. For abortion. I don't go for that." It was a position I could respect, but I didn't know what lay behind it. His mother and stepfather were Seventh-Day Adventists, I knew; was he complying with religious doctrine? Was he trying, as I was, to fathom some new radiance already dawning, unexpectedly, in his life? I only hoped that he wasn't trying to pressure Veronica into having the baby. "I can respect that," I said. "Just remember it's up to her. It's her decision." And I respected him as well for neither agreeing with me nor arguing, although his sigh and frown suggested he not only disagreed but was disappointed since we seemed to agree on so much else. He seemed unable to understand why I would offer up such liberal nonsense when I had the chance to become a grandfather, although, very possibly, that was my puzzlement, not his.

Kathi and I had of course been talking about the whole situation. I knew that it was different for her; she grasped it from a different angle. Veronica's first guess about her reaction was mainly correct, but Kathi had also felt an unexpected thrill, and she is a woman honest enough, emotionally true to herself, to admit it. "It wouldn't be so bad, you know, having a little baby in the house again!" Hokey or not, when we embraced then, I felt a bright convergence of some sort, a physical thrill that passed from chest to chest, augmenting what each of us felt with the other's unexpected delight, a commingling that created a new emotional reality that was not to be denied. For Kathi, a feminist professor at a women's college as well as Veronica's mother, pregnancy seemed to threaten our promising daughter's ascent, her ambitions, satisfactions, the contributions she would make in her profession. It was an old and tragic story, a societal trap that birth control had mostly rendered obsolete and in which the right to an abortion would ensure that a young woman remained in control of her destiny.

As for me, I have to admit to some resentment. I couldn't imagine how we could accommodate a child in our household. We had been thinking of moving. I had been looking forward to time with just Kathi, our parenting days over, the house our own.

And yet there was this undeniable excitement; maybe it was merely the exhilaration that comes when a well-ordered life suddenly goes off the rails, the feeling that accompanies the knowledge that life is about to change. It was hard not to see it in binary terms, two opposing forces that could be assigned the hero or villain role depending on your point of view. As Veronica said sometime not long after that, "There's no point in talking about it anymore. All your friends think I should get an abortion, and all my girlfriends want me to have the baby. I don't need any more talking with or talking to!"

Our ambivalence didn't make it easy for her while she tried to decide. On one occasion, after a conversation with a friend who conjured a vision I had suppressed until then, a specter I had sealed away, of Veronica alone in a housing project with several babies by different fathers, subsisting on welfare checks, I completely went to pieces.

We had fallen into a kind of pattern in which, on a daily basis, Kathi and I would try to assess where Veronica was in her decision process, then talk about it at night in bed before sleep, with books neither of us could concentrate on tented on our chests. I believed that if Veronica chose to have the baby, we would welcome the child, lovingly and joyfully, and help her, and Damion if he remained involved, and I kept telling her that, even as I pointed out that she could always have a baby later, when she was better prepared for it, when her studies were finished, when she was in a stable relationship, when it would cost her less. She was the first to get angry: "No! You can't have it both ways, Daddy! You can't say this and then say that. At least be honest about what *you* want. You're making me crazy!"

That night our tense arguing ended with my raging and roaring at her that she was not facing up to reality, that she was about to ruin her life. Even as I destroyed the image of the warm, calm paternal advisor I had wanted to be, I knew that I'd allowed my worst fears to assume control of my behavior. It took several days for Veronica to accept my apology.

"But why didn't she call me? I mean, I'm very happy for her, but what I can't figure out is why you're the one telling me this. Is everything all right?" Veronica was his only granddaughter and he doted on her.

"Well, I guess she wasn't sure how you'd feel about it."

"Why should she care what I feel about it? I just want her to be happy. Is she happy?"

"I think so."

"You think so? She's having a baby and you *think* she's happy?"

"It's complicated. I think she didn't know if you'd approve. I mean, first of all, she's not married."

"Oh hell, that don't matter no more. Not these days."

"And I guess because the father is Jamaican. He's black."

"Well, what difference does that make? For God's sake, you were never raised like that!"

I almost dropped the phone.

The first blow to my father's assurance that he still had what he called "a long ways to go" came with the news of his brother Francis's death in his early eighties. My father said, perhaps looking for an explanation, since their three older siblings were all healthy and strong and well into their nineties, "He was a bitter man. I don't know what happened to him, but he became a bitter man. I don't know. Did he strike you that way?"

"Well, he was a POW, after all. I don't think the Nazis treated their prisoners very well. Who knows what happened to him?" I also didn't think that his bitterness, whatever its source, accounted for his dying; there were plenty of bitter nonagenarians in the world.

"The only thing he ever told me about that was how, whenever a new commander took over the camp, he had to kneel down and pray in front of him. He had to say the Our Father, the Hail Mary and the Glory Be, with the translator there, I guess, to prove he wasn't Jewish. Francis had the Hoffman hair and he was pretty dark and Hoffman is a Jewish name. Except for that, I never heard him complain about it. But I guess that's not the kind of thing you talk about."

That's always been a long list in my family: "Not the Kind of Thing You Talk About." On it is the disappearance of Francis's daughter, Joanne. My cousin Joanne was my first love. Our babysitter, she made my brother Bobby and me laugh, think, wonder, and question. When we were small, before Bobby weakened and needed braces and then a wheelchair, she babysat when my parents went out to play pinochle or canasta with the neighbors. She always brought her portable record player that looked like a plaid suitcase and the latest 45s, and she danced and sang along with the Platters, Fats Domino, and Elvis. Soon we were doing it too, not dancing exactly but throwing ourselves around, goofy, laughing, just between imitation and mockery, weirdly uncomfortable but deeply pleasurable. We kept catching each other's eye as if to say we knew how weird this was but it was fun so who cares? I was too young to have a name for the charged erotic atmosphere of my cousin's innocent sixteen-year-old rapture, but I'm sure that even as a seven-year-old I took more than aesthetic pleasure in Joanne's thrilling femininity. Especially the night we sat at the kitchen table with her while she painted her fingernails: I had only ever seen my mother perform this ritual, with its alarming but pleasant smell, its fierce concentration, its thorough transformation of utility to beauty. If she was not already, or not quite, my cousin Joanne was becoming, joyously and giddily, a woman.

We each got a pinky, Bobby first. As she finished painting her thumb, Joanne showed us how to use the lip of the tiny bottle to remove extra paint and how to smoothly apply the bright red polish evenly, starting at the cuticle. I watched Bobby and I thought I could do better. I wanted to be better than Bobby at everything; I think that as his older brother I thought it was my job. Until soon after, when he began falling down, too weak to get up again, and I tried not to be.

I took a lesson here, I believe, from my father, who played card games and board games with us and only sometimes won. I began to suspect that if my love for my brother meant anything more than sleeping under the same roof (and in different rooms now that he was ill and in a wheelchair), then the exuberance of boyhood and adolescence would have to be tamped down somewhat, just as I would have to sit or kneel to talk to him.

But of course Joanne wouldn't set us against each other by playing favorite. I don't recall which of us had the idea to paint her toes, but she nixed that. I imagine we'd already done a sloppy job on her pinkies.

My mother called Joanne a tomboy, a word that I couldn't quite grasp because it seemed like a compound, and even if it meant a girl who was like a boy, I couldn't figure how the "tom" got in there. Joanne was no stranger to a baseball glove, and liked to play catch with us in the backyard, bringing her own mitt. Still, "like a boy" she wasn't.

And then she just stopped coming. If our parents were going out—usually to a neighbor's house or to my Aunt Kitty and Uncle Forrest's house for pinochle and beer—Bobby and I would jump up and down and yell, "Joanne! Joanne!" but it was always one of my other cousins, one of Aunt Kitty's daughters, who came to babysit. It wasn't that we didn't enjoy our cousins Annmarie or Maryann, it's more that we missed Joanne, and no one gave us any reason why she no longer came over to "mind" us or even visit. Our other cousins, Aunt Kitty's daughters, were sweet enough but would never wrestle or play catch with us.

I must have found out the way I found out most things, by eavesdropping on adults, probably listening to my parents' conversation through the floor register at night when we were supposed to be sleeping. My Uncle Francis had "thrown her out of the house." That's what I understood as a young boy. That, and the additional information that she "went to live with the coloreds."

It isn't hard to imagine Uncle Francis in a racist rage. I don't think I saw him more than half a dozen times over the next half century, but each time, somehow, he managed to insert the term "nigger" into the flow of the conversation, no matter what the topic. All through the years of the civil rights struggle, or watching Willie Mays or Hank Aaron or Elston Howard play baseball, or Wilt Chamberlain or Oscar Robertson play basketball, it was always nigger this and nigger that.

My uncle disowned his daughter, his only child. She was sixteen, maybe seventeen, still in high school where she met a young man who shared her taste in music, who treated her as the beautiful woman she was becoming, and who was black. Something happened then. My uncle saw them walking down the street together in one version of the story; in another, the young man beckons to her on the dance floor and she joins him and someone tells my uncle. What does it matter? We never saw her again.

I once tried to write a novel based in part on this situation, but I couldn't imagine the life of my cousin afterward, when the African American community took her in, recognizing her as a casualty of the same ugly racism they knew so well. I knew nothing of that life. It was a historical novel; no, worse, a costume drama. I could outfit the characters with garb and accents, always careful to avoid, offset, or subvert stereotypes, but I knew nothing of the ways, the understandings, the culture of black people in that place and time but what I could glean from books, magazines, and the Internet. It was all a put-up job and I abandoned it, having discovered that I was a liberal in the worst sense: I wrote my black characters just like all the other people I knew, white people. I wrote them in blackface.

How could it have been that I grew up in the industrial heartland and in a blue-collar neighborhood of mostly steelworkers and autoworkers—and still I knew no black people. How can that be? The answer to that question lies in the deeply internalized segregation that was the geographical expression of the hatred that had taken my cousin from us. Perhaps it was a liberation for her.

And I realize now, writing this, that my awful vision of Veronica alone and desperate and defeated is the American nightmare, generated and sustained by white supremacists like my uncle.

And my grandfather. My grandfather and his watermelon—it's a summer memory from 1954 or '55. My grandfather sits in his black leather chair by the window onto the alley, his cane hung over one arm of the chair where some of the horsehair stuffing is visible through a brown tear in the leather. Not long before, I'd had my hand slapped for pulling some of the long bristles from the slit. Now, Bobby and I are sitting cross-legged on the floor at my grandfather's feet in his high-top, lace-up shoes before half a watermelon and a long knife on newspaper. We're not allowed to handle the knife. My grandfather gives us each a slice of the melon and we watch as he eats his, making exaggerated sounds of delight, *Mmmm, mmmmnnnn.* After each bite, he spits the seeds out the window, which is shocking and comic and, we know, forbidden. Our grandmother would not approve. Five or six years old—I don't believe we'd started school— we love this moment. We're Pappy's trusted coconspirators, although we can't wait to run and tell someone, "Pappy spit the seeds out the window! Pappy spit the seeds out the window!" And as he does, he says, "Get out of here, black nigger!" *Too-ey!* "Get out of here, black nigger!" over and over.

Bobby and I do it, too, laughing so hard we almost choke. We both know we must not swallow the seeds; a watermelon will grow in your stomach. It isn't easy to spit out only the seeds. Bobby has bits of the pink flesh down his chin and I haven't mastered it, either. To be sure to get the seeds out

the window we stick our heads out. Bobby can't say his L's—
later he will get after-school help with this—so he says,
"Outta here, byack nicker. Outta here, byack nicker." We
mimic our grandfather, laughing and chanting and spitting
till the melon is a pile of ribs next to the knife on the newspaper. Our hands, our chins, our forearms are sticky with
drying juice.

Once when I'd asked him about Joanne, my father said that
the last he'd heard of her, somebody had said she was pushing a baby in a carriage. "The baby was white," he added.
"It was a white baby!" He shook his head as if to say that
my uncle had been mistaken, which made me wonder if
Joanne's banishment had been a response to a pregnancy,
and if my uncle had been led to believe that the baby's father
was black. My father seemed to think that it was a shame,
not that my uncle had disowned his only daughter, but that
he had done so needlessly: "It was a white baby!"

Beyond the murkiness of my cousin's story, there are
other questions that I despair of ever fully understanding.
How could my parents have gone along with this? Especially my mother. Joanne's mother had died while she was
very young, and my mother was without a daughter. Was
my mother so powerless to intervene? And how could my
father have acquiesced? Francis was his older brother; was
there some strict rule of primogeniture at work? "She just
disappeared," my father said, "poof! just like that. I think she
sent Kitty a Christmas card or a note once in a while, but
she was just gone."

When my uncle was on his deathbed in Florida, one of
my cousins thought she might be able to track down Joanne
by means of her most recent return address. "Do you want
us to try to find Joanne?"

"Joanne who?"

"Your daughter!"

"I have no daughter."

A short time after telling my father of Veronica's pregnancy, I sent him a photograph of Veronica and Damion sitting together on our living room sofa. At the time they were living in our house, along with our son, Robert, who had returned from Miami, where he'd been struggling in college. My father called to thank me for the photograph. "But she don't look happy," he said.

I dodged the invitation to candor, the first of several times I would do so. He was insistent, and right, of course. "I know my granddaughter, and she don't look happy." In fact neither Veronica nor Damion was happy. They were scared. They were fighting. They were on again, off again. They'd hardly known each other before the pregnancy, and now they were trying to learn how to love each other while living in our crowded house. So my father was, as always, perceptive, but I knew there was a racist element to his concern, and I wanted to be careful not to engage with it. I considered it a sleeping dog it would be best to let lie.

The next time I visited, soon after my father's diagnosis, I saw that he'd tacked the photograph up on the bulletin board beside his chair, which occupied the same spot, in the same room, by the same window onto the alley, as my grandfather's. When I mentioned to my brother that it was nice to see it there, Joe laughed. "When I got home from work the day that picture came, he handed it to me and asked me what I thought. 'Nice picture,' I said. And then he spilled it. 'But look at the guy. He's black!' I said that I thought we had established that. But he shook his head and kept saying, 'He's black. He's black!' I think he thought he'd be Derek Jeter or Obama or something. He figured he'd be brown, I guess."

Oh come on, you were never raised like that.

My father didn't know the half of it. I couldn't begin to tell him the complex truth of the situation. It saddened me, since we had for the past fifteen years or so been able to talk honestly about our lives. It had taken us both a great deal of effort to reestablish, some years after my mother's death, a communication beyond the sports and weather talk that had replaced, for decades, our lost intimacy. Now, once again, I had a secret I could not bring myself to share with him.

Damion, the smiling, broad-shouldered, warm, funny young man who lived with us, was a felon, recently paroled from federal prison, where he'd served time for dealing marijuana across state lines, and for gun possession. I watched his mounting discouragement as he tried to find work; day after day, following some lead, he would go off hopeful and come home sullen and sad. It was a tight job market, and employers wouldn't give a second look to anyone with a record. After several months he found work refurbishing electric meters. I helped him buy a car to get back and forth to the job. He seemed to be doing all he could, making every effort to turn himself into the father he'd never had.

But he was also facing state charges for gun possession, charges a good attorney would have folded into the previous court case. The court seemed to be stringing him along, continuing his case for more than a year as if ratcheting up the tension, month after month, to see how much he could take. He was about to start a family, and he could be plucked from his life at any moment and sent back to prison. We hired a defense attorney. I wrote to the DA. I spoke to my state representative. Damion and I spoke to a reporter who did a story on his case. Why, we argued, would the state want to resurrect this old charge? His offense had no victim and had taken place before he'd gone to prison. Why negate the changes in his life, changes that are the whole point of sending a person to prison? Why throw him away? Why punish a newborn who needed a father? We were fighting hard on his behalf. Kathi, Veronica, Robert, and I, along with several of our friends, wrote letters to everyone we could think of who might have some influence.

But I couldn't tell my father any of this; I knew very well what it would mean to him, what it would wake in him. Not long before, I had sat next to him watching, on his mammoth TV, a program called *Lock-up: RAW*, which as far as I could tell was a white supremacist's wet dream—and I'm using that term on purpose: the screen was filled with black men stripped naked and herded in a mass of flesh, past iron bars from one room to another, while a voice-over spoke of the warden's challenges keeping order and the guards' valiant efforts to not sink to the level of depravity of the prisoners. Whenever a prisoner happened to turn toward the camera, his genitals were hidden by a blurry disordering of pixels. "What the hell are we watching?" I asked him. "Let's find something else."

"You never seem to be able to completely civilize them." That's what my father said as he pointed the remote at the TV. My father who had been a counselor at the Boys Club in the black neighborhood in town. My father who laughed and smiled and greeted black friends warmly when we were in a bar or restaurant. My father for whom every black person he knew personally was an exception to the rule.

I could hear a strange, proud note in my father's voice when he talked about his illness. He kept saying that his body was shutting down. He liked to think of his bone marrow as a factory where red blood cells were produced. In addition to being proud, I think he felt somewhat relieved: he wasn't dying through any fault of his own. Like so many guys in that postindustrial rustbelt city, he was out of work, so to speak, but there was no shame in it—the factory, the steel mill, the truck plant, his bone marrow, had shut down. Nothing to be done about it. Not his fault.

Which suggests, to me anyway, that he still blamed my mother for her early death. It was her fault—three packs of Chesterfields a day—of course she would ruin her lungs. He had managed to quit. Why couldn't she?

He had not been overcome nor defeated: nothing had eaten him, neither tiger nor microbe. He was simply "shutting down." The sidewalk around the house was heaving and cracking with weeds in clumps. The chain-link in the yard was rusty. The whole place, the whole life, was shutting down. Nothing to be done about it. It's nobody's fault.

I was the one looking for an explanation, for a scapegoat. Aunt Kitty had died in her nineties, Uncle Eddie was still alive at the time, ninety-four or ninety-five, and Uncle Don, another nonagenarian, was out in Oregon. My father could have had at least another decade, if only he'd eaten better; if only he'd exercised; if only he'd been treated for depression; if only. I was the one who still needed to find the world reasonable, intelligible in some larger sense.

I usually called him Tuesday nights since he would have his lab results then, "my numbers," he called them. He had his notebook, a kind of scorebook not unlike the spiral bound books of box scores he kept assiduously during his years as a baseball coach, the notebook now filled with numbers tracing the rise or fall of platelets, hemoglobin, white blood cells, and so on.

There was something surreal about our phone conversations. That he was dying was acknowledged, and yet he was somehow invigorated by the struggle. It was as if this man, who had been a paratrooper in WWII, who had struggled to support a family that included two terminally ill sons, and whose wife had died nearly a quarter century earlier, recognized, even welcomed, his old adversary. It was as if this time, both fearful and curious, he wanted to get a good look at him, maybe get the chance to spit in his eye.

He wondered if death would come in the night, if it would come in his sleep. How much time do I have? He read his numbers for clues, charted their rise and fall from week to week, searched the Internet for explanations of what was happening to him. One Tuesday night when I called he seemed especially upbeat.

"So how are your numbers?"

"Pretty good. Pretty good. A couple of them went down but only slightly. Two of them even went up a little bit!"

"That sounds great. Maybe you hit some kind of plateau."

"That would suit me fine. I don't feel sick. I'm tired as hell but I don't feel sick."

"So what are you doing different?"

"I try to think if I changed my diet or something. I don't know. I'm eating a lot of chicken. Is chicken good for you?"

"Oh, sure. A lot of people swear by it. Chicken soup especially."

"Soup?"

"Yeah. How are you cooking it?"

"Oh, I don't cook it. Your brother brings it home. You know, the good stuff. The watchacallit, Colonel Sanders chicken. A couple, three times a week on his way home from work."

"KFC!" I laughed loudly. "Oh yeah, that's health food, all right."

"Well, it seems to be working!"

&

When Damion moved in with us, we were already a full house. Veronica had been living in her college dormitory for a semester but chose to return home and commute. Robert had been living in Miami, supposedly going to school; in fact, he had failed some courses, stopped attending others, was living on money we sent him every month, and could not bring himself to come clean with us.

We had all been worried about him for some time. A couple of years earlier, Veronica, then a high school student, went to visit him. At the time he was still enrolled at Florida International University. He had his own apartment and she was going to stay with him there. She called me crying.

"Daddy, you have to get him out of here! I don't know what's happened to him, but you've got to bring him home!" What she told me then, about multiple identities, different narratives of his life offered to different people, drinking, steroid injections, a complex web of feints and dodges, was frightening.

I had been sober nearly twenty years by then, and I felt sure that I recognized the frantic self-invention covering the sucking wound of addiction. And I knew that as the first-born son of an alcoholic, the odds of escaping some version of addictive illness were stacked against him. Still, I reasoned, he needed some room to find himself. I felt I had to be careful not to overwrite his story with my own, the easiest trap for any parent to fall into.

And yet, as the poor grades arrived, along with court

summonses for moving violations, for stacks of parking tickets unpaid, and for fender benders, I found myself awake and staring at the ceiling many nights, feeling helpless and worried. I only understood how worried I was when the phone rang at two in the morning—a wrong number—and after I hung up I realized I'd feared it was the Florida State Police.

Kathi and I met with a substance-abuse counselor, a former colleague from the years when I worked at an addiction and mental health clinic. He was an expert at staging and conducting interventions. He thought an intervention premature, maybe inappropriate. We all worried about overreacting. We needed more information, so we arranged to visit Robert in Florida. We spent a week with him. We took a trip down along the Keys. We returned home none the wiser and only a little less worried.

It would be another two years before the extent of our son's deceptions and the unsustainable webwork of his lies—the ones he told us, the ones he told his friends, and the ones he told himself—became known. He had recently rented an apartment with his oldest friend, who was in the Coast Guard and stationed in Miami. The friend called us one night. He spoke to Kathi.

"I'm worried about him. He doesn't seem to care about anything. He just hangs out with his friends or watches TV. He doesn't work or anything. It's like his life is going nowhere."

"Well, we don't want him working too many hours a week. He's been falling behind in his coursework and we want him to concentrate on school right now."

"School? Jesus. You think he's going to school?"

He had been quoting me, to the penny, his tuition, fees, books each semester. After his first year, he'd established residence in Florida: off-campus apartment, driver's license and registration, etc., because in-state tuition was much cheaper. I was depositing money—borrowed from home equity—into his account, along with an amount each month for his rent, utilities, and expenses.

Kathi and I were heartbroken and furious. She went online and bought him a one-way ticket home. We called him with an ultimatum: "If you want to continue to have a relationship with your parents, you will be on that flight." Did we mean it?

I called my father that evening. "Well, that's the last you've seen of him," he said. I didn't believe it but the prospect terrified me. I realized we were bluffing. Neither of us could have followed through on our threat.

Until then I had always thought of myself as the son in the story of the Prodigal Son. I was unprepared to play the father. Robert arrived at the airport. He was alternately flushed and pale, shaking and silent. I don't think any of us said a word either waiting at the baggage carousel or in the car on the way home. The whole edifice of lies now rubble, the next several days were a continuous wail of remorse, promises, confusion, grief. Racked by sobs, his head in his hands, Robert kept saying, "I don't know what's wrong with me. Something's wrong with me."

I called my father, relieved we had our son home, and angry about all the money he'd taken under false pretenses.

"That money's going to seem well spent if you can get that kid straightened out," my father said. "Don't be fooled. If you and Kathi handle this right, it could be your finest hour as parents. Just keep your eye on the ball. That boy needs you now."

Robert of course resisted the idea that he was addicted to alcohol. "I know that's your idea, Dad. And I appreciate your concern, but that's you, not me. I don't know what's the matter with me, but it's not that. In fact, out of respect for your recovery, I won't drink at all while I'm living with you guys. Not even a beer." And then one night he came home smashed and puked all over his room. From that moment on, he began rebuilding his life, seeing a counselor, going to 12-step meetings. There were times he despaired. "You can do this," I said to him, squeezing his shoulders, our foreheads touching. "You can do this."

I blamed myself. Why had I been so trusting and gullible? Why had we let him enroll in a school with thirty-eight thousand students when we knew he did best in a smaller, personally supportive setting? Why hadn't I responded with more urgency when I was so worried? Why do I talk myself out of things I know in my heart? It was my drunken behavior when he was still a toddler, my rages and inconsistent parenting before I sobered up, that had lain the groundwork for his suffering. I had passed this along to him, if not genetically—although that was likely—then by means of some behavioral or cognitive twist communicated by my early fathering. I had failed that beautiful child, and now this young man didn't know who he was and it was my fault.

You feel responsible. You're the parent. You can't help it.

The months of Veronica's pregnancy were tense. She and Damion mostly lived in her bedroom. Robert had committed himself to sobriety and was working hard to keep himself on an even keel. Kathi and I were both teaching full time, and I was also making extra money teaching in a low-residency graduate program. The house was a stressful chamber of unspoken worries, recriminations, angers, misunderstandings, and fear.

A friend reassured me, in a statement that now seems

prescient, "Babies bring their own joy, Richard. Just remember that. Babies bring their own joy."

The way I remember that morning is that I'd just gotten up and was making coffee in the kitchen, bleary-eyed and dull, as I am most mornings. The phone rang and Kathi answered it. I heard her scream. "Richard! Pick up the phone! Pick up the phone!" I grabbed the extension on the counter.

"Daddy!" It was Veronica and she was crying. Then there was a long and terrifying wail.

"What's wrong? Tell me! Tell me what's wrong!" I shouted into the phone.

It turns out those were my first words to the newest member of our family, who was being held shrieking to the receiver by his father, whose voice came next on the line, "It's okay, it's okay. He's just saying hello to his grandparents."

A month after his birth, Veronica went back to college for the final year of her nursing degree, and Damion cared for their son tenderly and joyously. Still, the pressures of the situation, including the possibility that Damion would be sent back to prison, were always with us. He found a job but it was minimum wage. As a nursing mother, Veronica was exhausted and finding studying difficult.

It was important to Veronica that my father meet her son, who was named after his father and after mine: Damion Richard Michael Smith. People assume that the Richard is for me. It's not.

Over the years, after the six-hour drive became too difficult for him, we had tried to get my father to fly up to Boston for a visit. No dice. As a young man, a soldier, he had flown on a number of occasions, but, a paratrooper, he had never landed, and he was resolved to have nothing to do with flying ever again. And there was certainly no question of his visiting now. His diagnosis must have felt like being kicked from a plane, and the following months like the descent: first panic and free fall, then the continual attempt to orient oneself. How to judge? Nothing but clouds. Once in a while a glimpse of the ground, the earth. But how much closer than last time? How fast am I falling?

So in March, during Veronica's spring break, she and I took the baby and headed for Pennsylvania. The drive down through Connecticut is always boring and often filled with delays until you swing west to cross the Hudson. More than once I had to come to a full stop, inching ahead for maybe a half hour, and then just as suddenly finding myself accelerating to a breezy 70 or 75 mph with no evident explanation. I called my father with a report of our progress. "No hurry. No hurry. I just talked to your cousin Maryann. Looks like Aunt Kitty's girls are coming over here tomorrow to meet your grandson."

After a few more hours, my grandson mostly asleep except when he was hungry, we crossed the Delaware River from Phillipsburg, New Jersey, to Easton, Pennsylvania. I believe that if you kidnapped and blindfolded me and left me in this part of Pennsylvania, I would know immediately on removing the blindfold where I was. The way the land rolls, folds on itself, promises the Poconos to the north, not to mention the Moravian stone barns and farmhouses, would give it away within moments. It's a landscape that continues west to the Alleghenies, and the closest thing I have to an ancestral home.

When I was a boy, our Cub Scout leader, Mrs. Steidel, took us to a vacant firehouse somewhere in town where a model train club had created a scale model of the Lehigh Valley Railroad as it had existed in its not-too-distant heyday. The men wore engineers' caps, which was one thing that struck us; another was that they did not patronize us but treated us as young people interested in learning about the geography and history of our region. Of course we were more concerned with, even awed by, the artistry of it all: the mountains, rivers, and ponds, the buildings. This was no flat platform under a Christmas tree with a train chugging round in a circle; this was a meticulous recreation of the world around us, with here and there a recognizable landmark to orient us. The scale was such that you walked through a landscape, thoroughly and minutely convincing, of rolling hills and shoulder-high mountains. Little Gullivers in Lilliput, we were larger and more suddenly aware of our increased stature than we would likely ever be again. A train whistle blew as a long freight train crossed the trestle over the Delaware near Easton bringing goods from New York; another brought coal through a tunnel in Union Gap, down from the coal regions near Wilkes-Barre. Brick factories; gray office buildings, including the PPL Building, our city's one jutting skyscraper; a train unloading cattle at the Arbogast & Bastian slaughterhouse on the Lehigh River. No acid trip I would ever take years later, no mescaline or psilocybin or peyote, ever made me feel so expansive, so able to encompass and contain and comprehend the world around me, as that art.

The overalled artists who guided us, necessarily single file, along the winding walkways of what was, for all its replicas of steel mills and slate mines and cement companies, a kind of Eden, were gardeners whose real crop was the people we blue, gold-kerchiefed, giant, and awestruck cubs would be one day. With their Casey Jones hats and red scarves, they pointed, elucidated, warned ("ah-ah, don't touch that") from their stations high above the mountains among the painted clouds.

&

I rang the bell and we stood waiting on the front porch, the baby, seven months old, riding high and curious in his mother's arms. Sometimes my father didn't hear the doorbell, so I went to the picture window, cupped my hands around my eyes, and peered in. I saw him rising very slowly from his chair and before he could turn toward the window I moved back to the door. I didn't want to suggest we were impatient with his slowness. I smiled at Veronica and touched my grandson's face.

When the door opened, after I'd taken in once again how pale his illness had left him, how utterly white he had become, and saw Veronica apprehend this and then erase it from her face, it struck me that we were four generations of a family together, probably the broadest span of generational time afforded anyone, and it felt like a kind of success. My father beamed and spoke first to the baby, who turned his body away and deeper into his mother's arms, but not his face.

"And who are you? What's your name?"

"Say, 'My name's Damion!'" said Veronica. "Hi, Pop-pop," and she kissed his cheek.

"Come in. Come in."

Inside the door my father clapped his hands softly twice and opened them to the baby who leaned from his mother's arms, happy to be held by this smiling man whom he'd not looked away from for a moment. Veronica touched my shoulder as if to acknowledge what we'd just seen.

My father handed the baby back to Veronica. "Just hold him for a minute, will you, honey?" He walked over to his chair, reached behind him for the arm of the latest incarnation of big recliner that has occupied the spot by the window since my grandfather's time, then pivoted and settled himself into the chair. I noted that beads of sweat had broken out on his impossibly white forehead. "Okay, now," he said. "Let me see that boy."

After a while we spread a blanket on the carpet with some of D's toys, his teething ring, a couple of rattles. My father got down on the floor to play with him. I wondered if that was a good idea, with his arthritic knees, his bad back, his sudden bouts of fatigue, but there was no stopping him. My brother Joe came home from work. He fetched a stuffed Penn State Nittany Lion from another room; battery-operated, it did a little dance and played the Penn State fight song. To my father's delight, the baby couldn't get enough of it.

It was hard to imagine where my father was getting his energy. For months, even before his diagnosis, his fatigue was the main symptom of his illness. I'm tempted to credit my grandson—*babies bring their own joy*—but it is more that D awakened a joy in my father that had lain dormant for a long time. I remember his delight with my own children when they were young. And before that, the way he delighted in my cousins' children. He was never entirely comfortable with infants, as if he were afraid to handle them too roughly, but once he could play with them, once they could respond to the faces he made, the tickling, the goofball sounds, the mock surprises, he would happily play the clown.

As my father hoisted himself up from the floor he looked at me and said, "That boy is all right." It took me several minutes to realize that what he meant was that he'd been examining him and there was nothing wrong with him, no muscular dystrophy.

The next day my cousins Elizabeth, Maryann, and Margaret arrived with what seemed like a truckload of gifts for the baby. They ringed Veronica and D, effusing and assuring her that they were there for her come what may. They passed the baby, who seemed to be enjoying his celebrity, from one to the other.

The entire time of our visit was passed in this positive, uncomplicated way, my father's numbered days notwithstanding. The baby seemed to nap when he did, as if they'd fallen into a shared rhythm.

And where was the baby's father? The official story was that he was working, was sorry he couldn't join us, would definitely come next time. A lie. Call it a white lie.

Of all my memories of that weekend, the one that will stay with me longest is the moment I turned round to see my father, sitting in his chair, planting a loud belly-kiss on my grandson's stomach, smiling from ear to ear, the tickled baby squealing with delight: my father with his black great-grandson held above his head, the two of them laughing, there by the window in my grandfather's chair.

An undertaker met me just inside the door and led me to a room where I could have some "private time with the deceased." Before she opened the door, she wanted to be sure that I knew that this private time was out of the ordinary but that they were glad to do it. "Yes, yes. Thank you." She opened the door.

One side of the door, the side toward me, was the rich paneled mahogany of the walls of the place, but when the undertaker closed the door, I saw the illusion: the door was metal-painted to look like wood; on this side it was painted a flat institutional olive like the rest of the store room. Gray steel shelves floor to ceiling were stacked with paper goods, supplies, cleaning products. Here and there on the floor were steel drums of something labeled with skull and crossbones POISON warnings. Daylight was filtered through frosted-glass windows and further baffled by the many tiers of shelved goods. Unlike the rest of the place, the room was not air-conditioned.

I stopped just inside the door. My father's body lay on a rusty metal gurney in the middle of the room, in the aisle between the shelves, covered to his throat with a stained yellow blanket. I was wearing a sport coat; leaving the house I thought I should wear a sport coat at least, even though it was what my father would have called a "stinkin' hot" day. Now the jacket added to the scene's absurdity. Why had I come here? I was losing my bearings. The room vibrated a bit and darkened from a truck going by in the narrow alley and I caught a little bit of salsa on the radio as it passed. There were sounds from within the building, too, on the other side of the door at the far end of the room, water running and, faintly, the sound of something like a dentist's drill. I looked at my feet, at my new black shoes. My father, it seemed to me, was waiting for me.

Earlier my brother and I had met with the funeral director, providing her with information for the obituary, picking the design for a funeral card. From the laminated pages of a three-ring binder, over and over, grisly images of the Crucifixion or the gates of heaven framed by billowing clouds. I chose the only one neither saccharine nor grotesque, a stand of trees with sunlight streaming down; on the reverse, the prayer of Saint Francis of Assisi:

> O Divine Master,
> Grant that I may not so much seek
> To be consoled as to console;
> To be understood, as to understand;
> To be loved, as to love;

For it is in giving
That we receive;
It is in pardoning
That we are pardoned;
It is in dying we are reborn
To eternal life.

"It's about the only prayer I can abide," I said. My brother nodded.

"Have you thought about a casket? I'll take you to our showroom when you're ready."

Whether I was stalling or needed to insist that I had at least some kind of spiritual life, or just needed to hear myself talk, I went on. "That's the prayer that was on the stained-glass window at St. Francis. I came on it years later in a different context and it made sense to me. I used to sit in church and look at that window. You know the one, Joe. St. Francis has his hands up—like this—and the sun is in the upper corner with the rays coming down and there are birds flying around and a little deer by his feet. I never understood why he had holes in his hands and feet until one of the nuns explained about the stigmata, how it was a miracle, that Francis was so Christ-like that he carried the bloody wounds of the Crucifixion. I used to wonder about that. It seemed so painful. Like if he was such a saint, why was his reward to be wounded like that? Later on, when I came across the prayer again, I saw it as a kind of step-by-step way to slip out of your ego. I don't think there's anything Catholic about it. Hell, the Church couldn't stand the guy while he was alive. They thought he was a pain in the ass." I thought I saw a look pass between my brother and the funeral director: *Uh-oh.* I could be wrong; in any case, I knew I was stuck in this monologue and had to finish it. I imagined the funeral director was used to people behaving weirdly in this situation, and my brother seemed similarly forbearing, so I went on.

"That's the thing all the mystics, the prophets, the saints, whatever you want to call them, all agree on, no matter what religion they come out of: you have to get past your ego, past what you want. It's a *technos*, a set of instructions. If you don't just say it, the prayer, if you stop at each separate point and really take it in, it's like reversing the poles of the usual, like an electric current or something. It's like life has us all turned inside out like a sock back from the wash, and the prayer is a set of instructions for turning yourself right side out again." Now they both looked concerned. I was concerned myself; I felt a little light-headed. And then a terrible self-consciousness gripped me. "Anyway," I said, and moved my hand dismissively in a way I instantly recognized was my father's.

"Can I get you anything? Coffee? Tea? Water?"

"Not for me," Joe said. I shook my head.

The funeral director rose. "Shall we go then? To choose a casket?"

Some were closed, some open. Some were wood. Some aluminum, some steel. Some were fine furniture: walnut, maple, cherry. Silks and satins inside: white, powder blue, silver, or rose. In only a moment I was overwhelmed. Joe asked, without quoting a figure, what she had in "a kind of midrange one." She showed us a deep-plum-colored steel casket with a buttery satin lining. And a muted silver model, blue inside. And a coppery one. I wasn't especially decisive, I just wanted this over with. "I think this one. What do you say, Joe?"

He shrugged, pursed his lips, nodded. We'd chosen the darker one. It had a little work where the railing was attached all around for the pallbearers.

"Very well then. Now, Richard, I understand that you would like to spend some time with your father?" I nodded. Back at her office she gave me a card. "Your father's at our other location, on Fourth Street. Do you know where that is?" I nodded again. "The address is there on the card. I'll call to let them know you're coming. You understand that our aesthetician hasn't finished with him yet, hasn't finished his work. I want to be sure you understand that."

It was perfectly appropriate that she was so businesslike and accommodating and I wished she was something more, although just what I couldn't say.

The other funeral home was across town, in a neighborhood near where I'd gone to high school. It was alive with bodegas, hoagie shops, travel agents, restaurants, fruit markets, and, at that time of day, kids coming home from school, the boys wearing ties and white shirts, the girls in their plaid Catholic jumpers. Whenever my father got on one of his rants about how the city was falling into ruin, my brother would tell him to come off it, that if he spoke Spanish, he'd think it was a great place to live.

I had been gripping an upright of the steel shelving, hard, a red crease in my palm. I moved toward my father. I touched his face and stood looking at him.

The expression on my father's face was odd, a kind of self-satisfied smirk. Maybe that's too strong a word, smirk. It's hard to describe because although I'd seen the expression thousands of times, it was always fleeting, the prelude to a wisecrack, or laughter, or his saying, "Aw, go on!" incredulously, a slight movement of the lip—except that now it wasn't a movement—on its way to something else. In the next instant surely he would say something.

&

The day before, I had set out as soon as my brother called to say that he'd taken my father to the emergency room. Traffic was heavy on the interstate. My brother called a couple of times to let me know what the doctors were saying. The next time he called he said, "Well, you didn't make it. And neither did he." The hospital staff wanted to know how far away I was and if they could move the body or if I'd be there soon. I said I was far away.

Alone in a car is a good place to get such news. I cried a good while, without restraint, before calling my wife and then my friend Will in Michigan, who loved my father like another son. He'd played baseball on one of my father's teams and had stayed close to him and our family for more than forty years. "The world is different now," I said to him. And then I spoke to my father, the one I'd made of him, the one in my head. Aloud. I thanked him and said good-bye.

As if he were ever going to go away.

I was trying to feel some of that grief now with all that was left of him in this stark room, but it was futile. A single fly, large, loud, came buzzing in a series of loops toward me, close enough that I shooed it away; it seemed to labor in the closeness and heat as it rose to a top shelf and alighted somewhere out of sight.

I was trying to orient myself. I looked away, scanning the shelves of plastic jugs and bottles, cartons, paper towels, not seeing anything. I wasn't feeling anything, either—no tears, no lump in the throat, no heartache.

But I recognized my state of mind. Had I been younger, had writing not been a part of my life for more than forty years, I would have panicked at my lack of emotion. I would have levied a terrible judgment on myself. But by now I knew that I was recording all of it, not only to write about it but to keep it, as I could not if I were distracted by sentiment. I knew I would weep again for my father, for his suffering, for the injustice of his life, for his loss. In that moment I was receiving a kind of imprint, as if I were recording a period of time, and a place, that would forever exist inside of me, a *camera oscura*, my time with my father's body in this room forever mine. I can return to that room now at will. I swear if I actually went back there I could tell you which cartons and containers had been moved. At any time now I can re-inhabit this storeroom pieta and I can grieve all I want, all I need.

The fly came humming toward me again and I ignored it. It alighted on my shoulder for a moment then zigzagged off toward the windows, where it bizzed along the frame and bumped along the frosted glass, looking for a way out.

Then I did something impulsive: I pulled the blanket from my father and stared. I began with his feet and noted where he'd torn off the nail of his big toe with a pliers a couple of weeks before; he'd bloodied it on the doorjamb in his bare feet, and trying to free the nail from where it had cut into his flesh, he tore the whole thing off. I looked at his bowed, arthritic legs and bony knees, his penis and—he had a dozen names for them—"the family jewels." He called them his privates. (Inflected with his army experience, the term became a quip, an adage: "Privates take orders; they don't give them." Good advice.) A hirsute man, my father's abundant chest hair came right up to his neck, and I could see that the mortician had shaved a little there, probably when told that we wanted to bury him without a necktie. And that smirk which made me want to say "What?"

It was not so much that I was looking at him; it was more my body, my whole body, recognizing itself in his.

It occurred to me then that someone might come in. What would they think? What would they think I was doing? *I* didn't even know what I was doing. I placed the blanket over him, kissed his forehead, patted him twice on the shoulder.

At the door I looked back at the body on the gurney, my father's body, the body we share. It seemed to mean, as surely as any broken bony Christ's down from his cross, "Don't be fooled. This is how it ends."

Except—suddenly I know it, wordlessly—it doesn't end. Don't be fooled.

Part Two

I imagine one of the reasons people cling to their hates so stubbornly is because they sense, once hate is gone, they will be forced to deal with pain.

JAMES BALDWIN

You arrive, take a number from a dispenser like the one at the deli counter of the supermarket, and fill out the yellow form on the counter in the back of the waiting room. Where the form asks my relation to the inmate I always write, in tiny print so it fits on the short single line, HE IS MY GRANDSON'S FATHER. I always feel a little exasperated that there isn't room for even that. Then you wait for your number to show up on the screen. The waiting room is full of people, mostly mothers and children. We sit in rows of attached chairs as at a bus station. There's a machine selling bottled water and sodas, another selling bags of salty snacks. I've been here several times before, but they've put up a wall since I was here last, a plywood wall with two Plexiglas windows that separates us from the main hall where the guards come and go, talking loudly, joking with each other as the shift changes. As time goes by, the children are more and more restless and their mothers, made up, with their hair done as if for a date, are becoming more and more frustrated, tugging arms, smacking bottoms: "I'm not going to tell you again!" Babies are shrieking and wailing. Every 20 minutes or so a guard calls out a handful of names of people who will be taken to the next phase of this process, allowed into "the trap" where they will take off their shoes and belts and step through a metal detector, then be asked to show there is nothing hidden under their pants or in their pockets. "Roll up your cuffs, please. Please pull down your socks. Turn around. Bend over. Stick out your tongue. Ma'am, if your child touches the bars of the gate again you won't be allowed to visit."

We are *les miserables*. The majority of us are black. Many of us speak Spanish. A lot of the women and nearly all the children are dressed in clothing with logos: GATORADE, DORITOS, NIKE, GAP. Lined faces topped with teased and dyed and sprayed bouffants, bad teeth, smokers' sallow complexions. Working people.

You have to put your belongings in one of the twenty-five-cent lockers, about a foot square. When my number appears in red dots, I go into the hall to the window to present my yellow sheet and identification. "You need to fill in your locker number." I've never had to do this before. He's going over the form, pen in hand. "Forty-one," I say. He hands the paper back to me. "You need to fill in the locker number, sir."

"Okay. May I borrow your pen a moment?"

"Pens are at the back counter. You know where they are." He refuses to meet my gaze. So I return to the waiting room and walk to the back counter, where I wait while people who've just arrived are filling out their yellow forms. A little girl is twisting around her mother's leg, bashful and curious, looking up at my exasperation, trying to puzzle out what exactly is going on here.

When I return to the window with a bold "41" in the box, the guard says, "They won't let you in there with that sweater on."

I've read the regulations. Several times. There's nothing else to read, nothing else to do once you've emptied your pockets and locked up your things. "Why not?"

"No vests. It's a vest." I'm trying to remember if there's

another quarter in my jacket in the locker. The guards don't make change. There's no point arguing with this guy. I walk away.

"You're welcome!" the guard shouts at my back. As I re-enter the waiting room, a running toddler, looking back at her older sister chasing her, slams into my knees, hard. She's crying on the floor and I reached down to pick her up, trying to soothe her. Her mother is there in an instant, snatching her away, while the older sister hangs back, twirling her hair around a finger. "Don't you touch my child!" the mother says to me. Everywhere babies are wailing, and now because I am the only drama in the room, all eyes are on me. There's no point in saying anything, so I mumble, "Sorry," and go stand against the wall next to the locker. There are no empty chairs.

An hour later, there are still many people ahead of me, and if I don't get in by four thirty, I'll have to wait until six. At last the guard calls Damion's name, and I get in the short line next to the iron door.

It took me a long time to finally visit Damion in prison. For one thing, I didn't feel I could visit him without a certain disloyalty to my daughter. She was ambivalent, given the fraught relationship they had at the time, and she said she didn't want to take D there because she felt that a prison was no place for a two-year-old. "But he remembers him, Dad. When we're out someplace and he sees a black guy with dreads, he asks me, 'Mommy? Is that my daddy?'"

After her first visit I asked her how it went.

"It was good. It was good. D sat on his lap and the two of them were playing around and laughing."

"I mean how was it for you?"

She teared up, resisted, then let loose. "I still feel it. In my heart. I still feel it!"

"You still love him."

She nodded as she blew her nose. And I knew that she knew how hard this would continue to be for a long time. After that, every Thursday evening she would take D with her and visit Damion in Concord.

My own resistance I still don't understand entirely. Even after my first visit, I made excuses. I made myself busy. The whole scene there is stressful for one thing, I told myself, and for another, sometimes I just don't know what to talk about with him. I don't really have an eventful life myself—mostly reading, writing, and teaching, none of which is of particular interest to him. It goes without saying that not too much is going on in his life. It's a little bit like visiting someone at bedside when they're in the hospital—it's just awkward.

But it is so much more complicated than that.

Soon after Veronica became pregnant, Damion moved in with us. Robert was also home, living in his old bedroom, just beginning to sort out his problems, engage in treatment for alcoholism, and recover from several years of self-destructive behavior. We were a full and uncomfortable house, all of us trying to get along, share limited space, and keep conflict to a minimum. I used to get furious when the strong smell of microwave popcorn or some Jamaican beef patties or jerk chicken would waft up to our bedroom when I was trying to get to sleep. And groping my way half asleep to the bathroom to pee in the middle of the night, I'd sometimes find a large dreadlocked stranger sitting on the toilet. "Jesus, close the door!"

"Sorry."

But I was impressed with Damion's solicitude and concern for Veronica's comfort during her pregnancy, his willingness to run downstairs to the kitchen or out to the store.

He rubbed her back, her legs. He soothed her anxieties. They seemed to me to be making a go of it.

Damion was looking for work. Each morning he would leave the house a young father to be, and he'd come home in the afternoon having been reminded more than once that he was a felon on parole. Not only that, but hanging over him was a three-year-old charge that, with adequate representation, not a court-appointed attorney, likely would have been dismissed. The state had decided to pull out that old file and prosecute him. Who would hire him? And how would he prove he was changed after his time in prison?

Around that time I went looking for a room to rent so I would have a place to write. I had a contract for a short-story collection, and I wanted to finish it. I had three stories in need of revision and three new ones in the works. I found a long triangular room in an industrial building and moved my desk, library, reading chair, and lamp into the space, just across the hall from an agency serving Salvadoran immigrants. I put my desk on one wall and a table against each of the other two. I have always written in multiple genres, and with my desk chair on wheels, and fiction, nonfiction, and poetry projects on their respective tables, I was able, whenever I felt stuck, to give myself a push and wheel across the room to a different work in progress. I mostly worked on the short stories and was grateful for the chance to escape the stresses of our life then: Veronica's pregnancy, the tensions of the household, Robert's crisis, my father's final illness.

That odd space became a haven, and I began to think. I would write for an hour and then sit there staring out the window for three. There had to be a way to have the charges against Damion dismissed. It was a matter of getting the DA to see him as more than a case, to see who he had become. I wrote the DA a letter and received a call from his office saying thank you, that the prosecution was carefully considering how to proceed. Kathi, Robert, Veronica, and others wrote as well.

For me, that time we were all together under one roof was too much like the household I had fled. We weren't fighting, but we weren't talking, either; we were mostly trying to stay out of one another's way. It was tense and lonely. And although the house I'd grown up in was filled with angers more chronic, tensions more constant, the two situations made a rhyme I wished I could erase.

For Kathi, that period reminded her of the year, early in our marriage, when we lived with her parents. We fought, I drank, both of us felt ourselves disappearing. Kathi would write until noon while I spent time with our newborn son. Then I'd hand him off to her and sit at the desk drinking and trying to write something. We were trying to bring two immense solitudes together, and we battled over temporal, parental, familial, and emotional boundaries. My mother was dying and I was flying back and forth to Allentown, leaving Kathi alone for days. Other times I played on her guilt to convince her to come with me so my mother could see her grandson. From one moment to the next Kathi was a mother, a daughter, a spouse—when and how would she also be a writer? Would she ever write again? Was she ever to have a professional life? One of her teachers, a poet, told her when she married that she was finished as a poet. Our life that year was mutual existential panic. Robert was our only joy.

And now he was back home with us, in his old room, which had been my study while he was away. In the parable of the prodigal son, there is no mention of the weeks and months following the moving scene of reconciliation, the father keeping his distance so he doesn't say the wrong thing, holding in check his resentment that his son is lying around the house all day, eating, sleeping, and doing not much else. The parable doesn't include the son missing his convivial pals and their nightly adventures from pub to bar to tavern. There is no mention of the son's girlfriend and how badly he wants to be back in her arms, no digression to examine the enervating effects of disgrace, how at such times it seems so clearly the opposite of grace, of comfort, of any ease at all.

We didn't know what to say to each other. He stayed in bed most of the day, watching DVDs on his laptop, and in the evening he would move to the sofa downstairs and watch TV. After Kathi and I went to bed, Damion and Veronica would sometimes join him.

I often wondered, boxed in my rented triangular room, if I would ever have my son back, the boy I once knew who was so buoyant and hopeful. Once, when he was ten or eleven, we were at Fenway Park and the Red Sox were down by nine runs going into the ninth inning. People were beginning to leave, had already been leaving for a while. I sighed, stretched, thought about the usual traffic jam in the sprawling parking lot across the street; maybe we could avoid it if we left now. Robert was standing in front of his seat, his fist in his mitt, ready for any foul ball that might come our way. I tapped his shoulder. "Come on, let's go. We'll beat the traffic."

"Dad, come on!" He gave me a look that accused me of treason. "Two grand slams and a homer and it's all tied up!" Now he was disconsolate, touchy, and evasive.

Robert is named after my brother Bobby. Kathi took my choice, my sad and sentimental attempt to thwart death, as the desire to honor my brother, but I did it more for my parents than anyone else. I wanted to assure them of the ongoingness of life. Lo! Your son who was dead is returned to you. Not only presumptuous, but useless: within eighteen months, my mother was dead, and my father devastated, isolated, depressed, and in retreat from life.

I fantasized about all of us moving to Canada. Maybe Jamaica. I never mentioned this to anyone; I just Googled the immigration requirements of countries where I thought we might all get a fresh start. I asked a writer I knew in Denmark, an American expat, how far we would get on the proceeds from the sale of our house. "You wouldn't make it out of the airport," he said. Kathi and I were too old; we'd be a drain on the system. "Maybe if you had a job you were coming for, or a corporate sponsorship of some kind." All I knew was that our daughter was starting a family with a man who was facing jail time for an old and victimless crime. The two of them appeared committed to each other, come what may. I had feelings too complicated to fully understand, but there were many things larger than my understanding in those stressful days, and fantasies and daydreams helped as a way to shepherd my thoughts away from the anger and confusion I felt.

I visited Damion every few weeks. Friends were puzzled. "Aren't you angry?" they'd ask. Of course I was angry. But at one remove from that heat there was warmth, familial, paternal, and also the memory of who I had been at his age: acquisitive, ambitious, desperate. I remembered the women I'd betrayed in the full-bore pursuit of my appetites, the need to prove I was what I then believed was a man. I remembered the thieving and lying, not to mention the drug dealing: the scale on the kitchen table, the bricks of marijuana in the closet of my Bronx apartment waiting to be measured out in one-ounce baggies. Who was I to judge? I often sat across from him in the visiting room, leaning forward, our elbows on our knees, staring at his broken teeth where a cop had bashed him in the mouth, and I thought of my own belabored and erratic coming-of-age, of my son's desperate flight from himself, and of my father's young rage. It was never clearer to me that the difference between our lives had been determined by the color of our skins.

&

There may be moments in childhood when some veil or shield moves aside and that instant is imprinted, stamped with terrific clarity on a region of the psyche usually occluded. It may have nothing to do with the force or importance of the persons or event experienced; it may have more to do with the condition of the child's consciousness: a lack or surfeit of sleep, hunger or satiety, anxiety or comfort. Who can say?

Discomfort with this puzzle leads some to a belief in fate, as if the soul is packing for a particular destination, its itinerary already known by some hidden faculty of the mind. I don't believe that. Still, it would be untruthful to say it has never *felt* that way, as if a part of me has been carrying certain of these high-definition memories as equipment, a subconscious education, a tutorial prepared especially for me. In any case, it surprises me that this memory is so sharp.

The rain had stopped. Puddles in the gutters swirled with the iridescence of oil. I was holding my father's thumb because his hand was too big, and he was taking me to the movies for the first time. It was 1954, I was five years old, and I had never seen a motion picture of any kind. We didn't have a television, although I had seen one in the window of a repair shop up the street.

There was a sign outside the theater, a vertical neon scroll that said ALLEN. Just outside the glass doors my father dropped to one knee in front of me, took my shoulders in his hands, and looked me in the eye. "You're going to be a good boy in there and do what I say. Right?"

I nodded.

"Yes, Daddy," he said.

"Yes, Daddy."

The carpeted lobby smelled wonderful, like caramel, like candles, like butter. The concession stand was a glass box of candy, along with something like an aquarium filled with popcorn. Some of the candy was "loose": horehound drops, root beer barrels, and the licorice my father bought me in a little brown bag. "A box of Jujubes for me," he said, "and a small bag of nigger babies for the young man." He rubbed my head and beamed at me in that way of his when he was showing me off, which was why I had to be good.

We went inside and as we walked down the aisle the lights dimmed. I stopped to see if it was our walking that was making it darker, then hurried to catch up to my father. Dim yellow and purple fluted lights along the walls cast soft fans of color upward, and there were golden vines and angels decorating the frame around a maroon curtain. My father had mentioned to me that before our church was built, the parish, St. Francis of Assisi, used to celebrate Sunday Mass here. The vaulted ceiling, the art deco light fixtures, the gold leaf, the deep carpets all contributed to a sense of the sacred. My father wanted to sit near the front. I liked the way the seats flipped down to sit on them, and I enjoyed that the seat cushion would go *whoomp* when I sat down and that it sprang back up when I stood. I did this over and over again until my father grabbed my arm and pulled me down. The heavy curtain was opening. The manic Warner Brothers music came up and a cartoon began, Bugs Bunny or Daffy Duck, probably. I can only recall eating my licorice and laughing with my father, watching the cartoon and see-ing my father throwing back his head to laugh. I laughed with him, laughed whenever he laughed, laughed because he was laughing.

When the cartoon ended, the music changed, and my father's mood changed with it. I tried to hold onto the hilar-ity we'd shared by recounting something from the cartoon, but he shushed me. The laughter was gone as quickly as if a faucet had been shut. The colorful cartoons gave way to a black-and-white landscape, and the sound of explosions. The music was dark and dramatic. I ate another piece of lico-rice and looked at my father for some cue how to react. He was slumped in his chair intently frowning at the screen, so I did the same.

Attack! was among the first Hollywood films to depict the grisly cost of war on particular soldiers. Two images from the film have stayed with me all my life. The first is of a tank crushing the arm of Lieutenant Costa, played by Jack Palance. Trapped in a doorway, the tank clatters loudly as he screams, his left arm smashed beneath the clanking treads. The other, from the end of the film, is Costa's dead body, his eyes open and staring, his head cocked back, chin jutting toward the sky. Together, they seem to have formed a statement I may not have been ready for: the first image, of terrible pain, I understood, at least in miniature; only some months before, I had caught my fingers in a door, and the intensity of that pain had me screaming and hysterical and for a long time beyond the consolation of my parents. The second was wholly new, an image of horror that tore through the soft flesh of my limited understanding. I knew the word "dead." I had some vague notion of what it meant. You went to heaven. But Costa didn't go to heaven, he just lay there on his back, mouth open, and my stomach churned black licorice and threatened to empty itself on the seat in front of me.

Recently I watched a VHS tape of the film. What struck me watching the tank scene was how clearly fake it was: Palance's arm buried in a hole in the ground, out of view, with the tank tread over it. But by then you're so adrenalized and panicked by the previous moments when the tank closes in on him, trapped in a doorway, pounding his shoulder against the wooden door and yanking at the knob until it comes off in his hand, that the tank crushing his arm, or perhaps worse, is already in your imagination—you've already conjured it from the depths of fear: of entrapment, of the existential moment of no escape.

But Palance's dead visage: even viewing it as an adult, even knowing it was an actor playing a part, did not dispel the stark horror of that death's head.

What does a child know of special effects? Those are corpses, not sprawled actors covered in syrup. A child has no disbelief to suspend, willingly or not. Besides, every detail in a film is meant to override the suspension of disbelief, every moment, every word, gesture, costume, and shadow is meant to convince.

I was convinced. My whole body was convinced.

Before that day I lived in the dream world of childhood: I spoke to worms and bumblebees, birds landed on the backyard fence and cocked their heads so quizzically I understood their queries. My brother Bobby and I ate rose petals and onion grass, and we lay on our bellies on the concrete walk in the sun because it was warm and felt so good. We were creatures, and although there was certainly a difference between sleeping and waking, it is also true that in another sense we lived in a more or less continuous dream. Even our father's rages, when he cursed and broke things and drew his belt from his pants and doubled it and forced us to submit to a "lickin'," were experienced as nightmarish disturbances within that dream. I don't mean to speak for Bobby, dead now forty years, and yet that was how it was with us then: born a year apart, we were not merely inseparable, we were hardly separate people at all.

It could be that we are all born into this dream, and that it is continuous and unending, even though soon, whether gradually or suddenly, we're separated from an awareness of it.

&

We were having a party in the backyard for D's first birthday. Veronica had done up the patio with a brightly colored tablecloth and about a hundred balloons she filled from a helium canister she'd purchased. Most of the guests were my grandson's family who live close by. Damion was in the county lockup awaiting trial on gun and drug charges. Veronica had been cooking all night and into the morning: curried chicken, shrimp, beans and rice, pasta with meatballs and sausages, salad, potato salad; and as if he knew something was going on, D had hardly slept.

By three in the afternoon the yard was filled with uncles, aunties, and cousins, a few neighbors and friends of ours, and a dozen kids racing around. One of the uncles had brought a bubble machine that sent thousands of bubbles the size of Ping-Pong balls wafting across the patio to the great delight of the littlest ones who chased and whirled and laughed. They couldn't get enough of it, and the machine had to be replenished with "bubble juice" several times.

Kathi, whom all our guests that afternoon, no matter their age, called Grandma, had D on her hip, and although he'd been cranky, he was laughing as he swatted at bubbles, his grandma exclaiming whenever he popped one.

I was standing on the deck where a buffet, including birthday cake, waited under plastic wrap and aluminum foil. I was watching Kathi, marveling at her ability to so thoroughly give herself to her grandson and enjoy the other kids who were drawn to her enthusiasm—"Look at me! Watch this!"—jumping up and down around her. Only three days earlier, she had been diagnosed with "ductile carcinoma in situ," or DCIS—breast cancer.

I try to remember the moment she told me. It must have been in the kitchen. Yes, I seem to recall hearing the news there. But this moment, her dancing around with the baby amid balloons and bubbles and leaping children, is the moment that stays with me. I've referred to my journal to refresh my memory of hearing the news, but there is no mention of that conversation per se; there is only fear and self-pity. I wrote as if I were being given the news my father received when my mother was diagnosed. I suppose I was primed to feel this way, and my fear of losing Kathi was terror commensurate with my love for her but, goddamn it, all I find written there is about me. I kept thinking I'm going to lose her; I'm going to lose her. Not once in those pages did I reflect on her feelings, on what her course of treatment would exact from her, or even on how I might make myself useful to her.

So the reason I keep returning to this memory of standing on the deck watching her is that it is kinder to me than recalling my selfish fear. But it is also true that the beauty of that moment pierced my numbing anxiety with a sudden, refreshed appreciation of her bravery. I have been witness to, and often beneficiary of, this courage for thirty years. I am not entirely joking when I quip to friends that by contrast I am a big baby, "You know me, if I get a haircut, I need to take a day off." And even though, later, she will say that she always knew there was no need to worry, I can't help but know how terrified and self-centered I would have been in her situation.

Veronica came out of the house with paper napkins, plastic knives and forks and cups. "It feels like rain. We'd better eat soon. Dad? Hey, are you okay?"

"Me? Yeah. Fine."

"Don't worry. You don't need to worry."

"I'm not. I know. I'm not worried."

Evidently, I wasn't very convincing. She made a face at me. Then she pointed into the crowd of kids where Kathi was pointing at me, talking to D, "Wave to Grandpa! Say, 'Hi, Grandpa!'"

"Maybe we should take the food inside," Veronica said. The wind was coming up, flapping the corners of the tablecloths. Somehow one of the balloons came loose and, after catching a moment in the leaves of a maple, soared higher and higher with the kids running up on the porch to see better as it gradually became a mere speck in the sky. Clouds were rolling in and it looked like rain.

"I want to do it!" yelled one of the boys, and he began tearing a balloon from a bouquet tied to the porch rail.

"Me too! I want to do it!" another boy called out. The younger kids had gone back to chasing bubbles.

The boys especially were riled up. Everywhere the balloons were fastened—to the deck, to the tables and chairs— the boys were tearing at the ribbons to free them.

"Hold on," I said. "Hold on! Wait! Wait!" Pouts on their faces, some anger on the faces of a couple of the older boys;

of course, they seemed to think, *of course some adult would put a stop to this much fun.* But I only wanted to slow things down. I knew this kind of energy; it threatened to sack the whole party and destroy the whole afternoon, especially for the youngest kids. "All right. Okay, listen up. You can each have one. One."

Kathi was giving me a look that asked if I had utterly forsaken being a responsible adult. I could see in my mind's eye the very Sierra Club photograph she was silently referencing with her loud frown—that pathetic Canada goose, starved, its beak clamped shut by a piece of a red rubber balloon. One of the girls pointed to the sky where the first balloon had all but disappeared. "It's going all the way up to heaven!" she shouted, jumping up and down and clapping. She gave me an idea.

Earlier that afternoon, a couple of hours before the party, Damion's father, Smithy, had arrived with a young woman about Veronica's age whom he introduced as his girlfriend. "We are the grandfathers!" he shouted as if making a pronouncement. He hugged me, clapped my back. It was easy to fall into a boisterous familiarity with him; easy for me, anyway. Kathi came into the hall and extended her hand in a way that was gracious but discouraged his loud assumption of his place in our lives. She was mindful of things that we knew about Smithy, things the volume of his presence had momentarily driven from my mind. Damion's mother was fourteen when he was born in Jamaica. Smithy was somewhere about thirty. Now here he was with this young woman who had yet to say a word or even make eye contact. At least she seemed to be of legal age.

Not long after Damion's birth, his mother's family sent her from Jamaica to the United States to continue her education. Damion was left with Smithy. I have since learned from Damion that he was beaten by his father, locked in his room in the evenings while his father went out, and made to carry his father's gun in his backpack and stay within easy reach. When Damion was seven, he asked if he could please live with his great-grandmother. According to Damion, Smithy was happy to be rid of him.

Although I did not think the occasion granted him a plenary indulgence, as Smithy apparently did, I felt it was a special moment, an instance out of the ordinary, and I wanted to be welcoming. Besides, the rest of Damion's family had not yet arrived, and I thought I should take my cues from them.

I needn't have wondered about that. Not one of the women—not Damion's mother nor his aunts nor members of his mother's church—would be in the same room with Smithy. If he walked in, they would simply turn their backs, excuse themselves, and leave the room. But it would be a long time until any of them arrived. We moved into the kitchen.

"I have brought to you the famous kukoomba juice! I make the juice for all Jamaica!" He held up a plastic gallon jug of green liquid. "The juice of the kukoomba make you strong! Down there! Strong! I don't need no Viagra. No!" He turned to the young woman who was standing just inside the doorway, looking at the floor. "Tell him!" She seemed to curl into herself and shrink. "Tell him, I say!"

"Excuse me," Kathi said, moving to the young woman and taking her by the arm. "Come. Come into the living room where we can sit down and talk." She asked the woman her name.

"Anything that is wrong for you, the kukoomba juice will cure it. Even good for the cancer. You try it. This I made special for you the grandfather. Try it!"

I went to the pantry for a glass. The juice was tasty, a clean fruity taste, sweetened with honey. "The drug companies, they want to shut me down. I make the juice for free, give it for anyone who is sick. I don't take no money, so they want to shut me down."

"Delicious," I said. It was. I poured myself a full glass this time.

"Ah, because you are the grandfather. I will give you how to make it. I will teach you."

Robert had come downstairs and was standing in the doorway. I poured him half a glass. "Here. This is my son, Robert. This is very tasty. You'll like it."

"No. No, thanks. I'm good."

"Robert. Smithy. Damion's father." They shook hands.

Then, as if I had just reminded him that he is Damion's father, Smithy said, "I brought him up to be a good man. I have told him, 'You have disappointed me. I taught you to do the good, not to do the bad. Why must you do the bad?'" In a transparent play for fatherly solidarity, he leaned toward me and said, "The young men, they don't listen. You try to teach them, but they do not listen to their fathers."

Robert was hanging in the doorway, and the look on his face asked, "Is this guy for real?" I was thinking of a five-year-old boy, walking next to his father, alert to his displeasure, staying close, with a pistol in his Flintstones backpack.

"First you need the good water. Spring water. In Jamaica the water is purest of anywhere, of any place. And then you must have the good kukoomba."

"Where can I get that?"

"All the markets, they have the kukoomba. The best kukoomba from anywhere in the whole world is in Jamaica."

"And you must make one gallon of water to five large

kukoomba. This you must do right. And you mash the ku-koomba with five tablespoons honey. Good honey . . ."

"I won't remember this. Here," I said and handed him a pad and pen we keep by the telephone. "Write down the ingredients for me."

"Yes, yes. For you, grandfather."

I watched him write it:

C-U-C-U-M-B-E-R

"I have a good idea!" I said to the kids. They gathered around, holding tight to their balloons. "Before we send our balloons up to heaven, why don't we each make a wish?"

"Yeah! A wish! A wish!"

"Will it come true?" one boy asked very earnestly.

"If you tell me your wish, I'll write it on a piece of paper and maybe when it gets up to heaven an angel will see it and read it." I was far out on a limb now. I had only meant to slow things down while keeping them interested. "Like, my wish is for D on his birthday. I want him to grow up big and strong and have a good life." I wrote "A Good Life for D" on a small piece of paper, rolled it up, tied it in the ribbon of the balloon, and let it go. We watched it rise. The adults stopped their conversations and watched, too. "Now me!" said a girl of five or six. "I want a girl baby cousin!" I wrote it and we launched it.

"Me! Me! I want a Xbox!" a boy said, bringing me his balloon. I asked him if he wanted to make a different wish, for something that would make life better. "A Xbox! A Xbox!" he insisted. I wrote it as the first drops fell from the sky and we sent his balloon up into the rain. Soon it was coming down hard, the adults scrambling from their chairs to herd the kids indoors.

"No, Mommy! No!" the boy cried. He sat down. His mother dragged him up by the arm as he twisted and yelled, "No, Mommy!" looking at the sky. "My Xbox! My Xbox!"

"Child, what are you talking about? Hush up that nonsense right now and get in that house."

In the steamy house he huddled in the corner, arms crossed on his chest, sulking and glaring at me as if I'd played a cruel trick on him. Later on, talking with Veronica, I learned that the boy's father is a quadriplegic, the result of a drive-by shooting that left him with a severed spinal cord, and I wondered what, in the childhood realm of magical thinking, that Xbox meant to his son: the sky must have seemed awfully low to that boy, the future so close that it hardly existed.

Sometime during that downpour, Smithy and the young woman slipped away without a good-bye.

My father died later that same week. The last e-mail I received from him suggested that Kathi might want to call my cousin Elizabeth, who had been successfully treated for breast cancer. He sent along her e-mail address and phone number.

&

When I first began to think about having gone to that film with my father, the question that seemed obvious was, of course, Why would a grown man—my father was twenty-nine at the time—take a five-year-old child to see such violence? And even though that's a good place to start, it presumes a great deal. It is unlikely that my father knew the content would be so graphic. War films to that point were not realistic and violent portrayals of battle. Especially during the war, Hollywood refrained from portraying the horror and gore that *Attack!* did not shy from. I also wonder if he had any idea at all that the film would be disturbing to me: his first-born, I was the only five-year-old he had ever known. The youngest in his family, he had absolutely no experience caring for a child. Otherwise, perhaps, he would have broken the film's spell, gathered our things together, and taken me out of there. These things matter. They must be considered. In those days my father was a counselor and coach at the Boys Club, where he was saturated in his all-male world of leather and liniment, wrestling mats, boxing rings, basketball courts. I think that he couldn't wait for me to be old enough to stop being a child and be a boy, or a "young man." None of this would have been conscious or intentional on his part.

Palance was my father's favorite actor. "He's from Hazleton, up the coal regions," he always said, jerking his thumb over his shoulder as if the coal regions were right behind him. The actor was in fact from Lattimer, a neighboring town in Luzerne County, site of the Lattimer Massacre of 1897, in which sheriff's deputies killed nineteen striking miners and injured forty-nine others. My father's people were from "up the coal regions." My grandfather, born in 1890, had been a "breaker boy," which meant that he went to school until he was ten, and then into the mines, where he spent his boyhood on a wooden bench in the colliery, beside a coal chute twelve hours a day, breaking coal into lumps of somewhat uniform size, and chipping away slate, shale, and other impurities with a hammer. My grandfather's entire coming-of-age took place in the mines. He grew into an apprentice, a journeyman, and then a master miner with his own crew. My grandmother was a miner's daughter. Together they began their family in a company house, buying from the company store, trying to stay a step ahead of the systemic and deliberate local inflation that trapped so many, managing to save a little money. When my grandfather narrowly survived a mine explosion that killed the members of his crew, losing his hearing in the process, my grandmother had had enough and insisted he forsake mining. They moved to Allentown, where my father was born, and they opened a small bread store there while my grandfather's hearing was slowly restored.

The "breaker boys" are usually credited with starting the rebellion that gave rise to the United Mine Workers union and the subsequent strikes that resulted in the massacres at Lattimer and elsewhere. These boys, hard as the anthracite that blackened their hands and faces, were also the most visible and shocking example of the child labor practices of the time. Their plight galvanized activists and politicians to write the nation's first child labor law in the early years of the century, a law that was overturned by the Supreme Court, which ruled that children had a "right to work." In fact, it was only when the Great Depression resulted in adults competing for those jobs that legislation placing restrictions on child labor was passed.

I recall sitting quietly with Bobby in my grandparents' living room with my father and uncles while my mother, grandmother, and girl cousins remained in the kitchen, cleaning up after supper. Impossible to remember what the men talked about—although I was thirteen when my grandfather died, these memories, which seem to have rolled themselves into one big representation, are from earlier. I know because Bobby is with me and he is not in a wheelchair. The overarching feeling, for which the deference and respect of his four sons is the only evidence I have, was that my grandfather was a very important man. I thought he was the governor of Pennsylvania probably, but maybe of the whole world, because that's how my father always addressed him. "Howdy, Governor," he'd say.

Or maybe I was impressed by the simple fact that he sat in his chair by the window and did not rise when my grandmother greeted us at the door. You went to him at the beginning and end of every visit; he did not greet you or see you out. There was a reason for this: my grandfather's legs had been shattered in a fall from a scaffolding, and it was hard for him to rise, get his two canes securely in hand, and get going. He wore high-top leather shoes for support. At least once I saw his bare leg, a shiny purple, swollen as a sausage about to burst. Reasonable as it therefore was for him to stay put, to me as a boy it lent him the air of a chieftain, especially with my father and uncles, all grown men, seated before him. Whatever the topic, they always seemed to be reporting to him.

It goes without saying that he didn't drive. Because we lived closest, my father was often the one to drive him to appointments. I recall one time we were driving along Front Street, by the river, near the two breweries and the slaughterhouse. It was poor. It smelled poor. It looked poor. It was chaotic, ragged, broken. Concrete steps crumbling away to gravel; screen doors rusted and torn. An immigrant neighborhood, port of entry to Allentown, it was Greek, Hungarian, Polish then, with some Syrians and Ukrainians, too. Riverfront Park with its three baseball diamonds, its bathhouse for swimming in the river, its basketball and handball courts, cushioned the length of the neighborhood. It was playing in that park, the smell of hops and barley thick in the air, along with the stench of flesh becoming meat, that forged forever in my mind a connection between poverty and slaughter.

We crossed the tracks into an area called Trout Creek,

into the "colored" neighborhood, more row houses, with here or there a lot filled with rubble. I gawked from the rear window of the car. There seemed to be a lot of people hanging around. It seemed crowded, uncomfortably so, and quiet, very quiet, as we passed by. Silent blank stares.

"Damn niggers breed like rabbits," my grandfather said, "they'd just as soon slit your throat. You keep that window rolled up back there and your car door locked if you don't want your throat cut." It took me both hands, panicked, to roll up the window.

It has taken me much of my life to roll it back down.

Could my grandfather have believed this? Could he not see the overcrowding for the confinement it was? And was this fear a twisted sort of empathy, an acknowledgment and understanding of the rage he imagined seething in that neighborhood?

Recently I was driving through Vermont with a friend, a German painter and photographer. I didn't know her well. Letta and I were both month-long residents of an artists' community, the Vermont Studio Center. Every so often she asked me to pull over so she could take a photo: of a covered bridge, of a tumbledown barn, of one of those sun-filled valleys that suddenly opens up around a curve in the road. Sometimes, a little unsure of her English, she would ask me if she was using a word correctly. "Do you say in English 'transverse'? This piece that goes across the top?" She had just taken a picture of a covered bridge. "Ah. So. I think this transverse must have been once a very tall tree." Other times, I could tell I had used some colloquialism that threw her. She asked how my work was going.

I told her the writing was slow, that I had the feeling I needed more information. I said I was trying to understand how my grandfather became such a racist. I wanted to understand him in the context of his time and place. I didn't think his lack of education had much to do with it, I said. Certainly I have met many educated racists. I wondered if it stemmed from competition for mining jobs. I figured that as freed slaves moved north in the decades following emancipation, they affected the labor market, perhaps at a time when workers were beginning to organize successfully. I said I was looking into that, but that I wasn't sure. I knew from my researches that the Ku Klux Klan was quite strong in Pennsylvania in the early years of the twentieth century, but my grandfather, being the son of Catholic immigrants, would more likely have been a target of their hatred, so I was barking up the wrong tree there. I said I was trying to understand the attitudes of the time and place in which my grandfather was steeped. "It's very puzzling to me," I said. "My family liked to tell stories of my grandparents inviting the homeless to their table for a meal during the Depression. Clearly none of their hungry guests were black. I just can't grasp his hatred and fear. I'm trying to understand where it came from."

Letta was silent long enough that even though the road was winding I turned my head to try to read her, prepared to clarify if I'd used an expression she didn't understand. She was glaring down at the camera she held with both hands in her lap. Her chest was heaving. I glanced back at the road, steered.

"This is nonsense!" she blurted. "I'm sorry, Richard, but I have heard these excuses, all of them, for the whole of my life. This is nonsense! The times. The circumstances. A person always has a choice: you either respect people or you turn them into the other. My parents were both Nazis. They were Nazis! There are no excuses. There is always a choice." She brought her knuckles to her mouth and stared straight ahead. I looked back at the road just in time to stay on it.

I wanted to protest but I could not disturb the silence that had filled the car in the wake of her vehemence. I wanted to argue that a person is shaped by his or her times as a tree is shaped by the weather, and that in fact the kinds of trees that grow in a place are determined by the climate. But I drove along, hugging the curves, wondering instead about analogies, about whether and when they turn into excuses, and I couldn't say a word.

I remember my grandfather's wide silk neckties. After my grandfather died, my father gathered them up and hung them in a clump on a hanger in the bathroom closet. They were my grandfather's pride, the coup de grâce of his sartorial elegance. I have no idea if his clothes were fashionable, only that my grandfather loved to dress in a suit and a fedora with a white silk lining. I think about it now and imagine my grandfather in front of a mirror, knotting one of his extraordinary ties, saying to himself, "Not bad for a breaker boy, by God, not bad for a coal cracker." The ties were nearly six inches wide and embroidered with birds, butterflies, and flowers that might more likely adorn a kimono or a Mandarin robe. I remember studying them, trying, before I had any tastes to exercise, to decide if they were beautiful or garish, vibrant or too loud. "Don't be fooled," my father said. "These are bound to come back in style. Just you wait and see."

What I've been told is that my grandfather fought in World War I. But I don't know anything about that, and growing up I knew little about that war. When my grandfather played his cherry wood Edison Victrola for me, with the little handle to wind the turntable, I heard:

Over there! Over there!
Send the word, send the word to beware.
The Yanks are coming,
The Yanks are coming,
The drums rum-tumming everywhere.
Over there! Over there!

The music always seemed a little fast, just like the early movies I sometimes saw on TV or the newsreels they still showed sometimes before movies. The records were as heavy as diner plates. It occurs to me now that this song is our real national anthem, or ought to be, embodying America's true relation to the rest of the world.

I once asked my father if he had any idea what lay behind my grandfather's racism. "Racism? Oh, hell, he hated everybody." He picked up the remote to let me know this would be a short conversation, reached down, yanked the lever on the side of his chair, and reclined. "I stopped trying to figure my father out a long time ago." And the look he gave me before he turned on the TV suggested that I ought to just grow up and do the same.

Impossible. My fascination, my obsession, with my father, with who he was and where he came from, what he thought, felt, and believed, has been constant throughout my life. At least since the day we walked out of the Allen theatre in a silence that lasted all the way home, I have wondered at him and the world as he understood it.

When I was nine, the American Legion baseball team my father coached won a championship, and instead of the traditional championship jackets he offered them a weekend trip to New York. I was the batboy so I got to go, too.

My father's car, his first, was a black Pontiac that sounded like a machine gun if you drove faster than 25 mph. On our way there we had to stop several times to let the radiator cool and get water. One of the players in the car—we were traveling in a caravan with the other coaches and with one or two of the players who had cars—said something about pissing into the radiator and everyone laughed. I laughed along but wondered if that wasn't a good idea since I had to pee and was afraid to ask if we could stop.

"We are under the river!" my father blurted as we entered the Holland Tunnel. Holland was a country, I knew from school, that would be entirely underwater were it not for the windmills and dikes that held back the sea, so the name of the tunnel made a nine-year-old's sense to me.

The parking garage for guests of the Prince George Hotel was a huge machine that seemed to work something like a Ferris wheel. The attendant drove the Pontiac into a steel mesh cage, and another man pressed a button and sent the car up, up into the building until we couldn't see it anymore, and several other cars in their cages came into view. I recall the smell of the garage, the exhaust fumes, the layers of grease and grime in the machinery, but there was nothing ugly about it; it seemed elegant to me and brilliant, my first understanding of the verticality of New York, which became almost unbearably exhilarating looking uptown to Thirty-Fourth Street, where the Empire State Building, which my father claimed was one of the seven wonders of the world, stood in its impossible glory.

Everything was a wonder to me on that trip and there's hardly a point in recounting the wide-eyed provincial kid arriving in the metropolis, but as we headed for Yankee Stadium that afternoon, I saw poverty more abject than any I'd seen in Allentown. Its hopelessness struck me with something like the vertigo I felt looking up at the skyscrapers of Manhattan, as if there were a pit exactly as deep as the Empire State Building. I saw kids my age, clothes shiny with grime, rags really, scrambling over piles of bricks in an alley, people hanging around doorways, leaning against walls, sitting on the front steps of buildings. Black people. I'd never seen so many black people. I was morbidly fascinated and wondered what was wrong with them; didn't they know how to live?

All it took to ratify my parochialism, my naive self-centeredness, my—say it—my racism, was the black man I saw drunk on a subway platform; right under a sign that said No Spitting, he hawked up a green wad and—*och-tooey!*— spurt it on the tracks. Then he glared at me. He was disgusting, dirty, perhaps dangerous. I stepped close to my father. Soon we'd be at the ballpark where Mantle and Maris would team up to clobber the opposition, where my father had promised to "buy me some peanuts and Cracker Jack" like the song he'd taught me when I was three.

"What a beautiful day for baseball!" My father pronounced as we emerged from the subway.

That afternoon, Mantle hit three homers in a double-header, one in the first game and two in the second. I don't recall who the Yankees played.

We drove home at night; it was cooler and the radiator didn't overheat. I sat in the back, hanging out the window, looking behind us at the skyline as it receded. Over and over, the song I heard everywhere during the weekend replayed in my ears, Harry Belafonte's "Banana Boat Song": *Come Mister Tallyman, tally me banana. Daylight come and me wanna go home.* When I could no longer see the skyline, I pulled my head back inside the car, resolved that I would live there one day.

I looked at the Yankees pennant I was bringing home for Bobby, and imagined telling him about the game. It was always tricky because while he seemed to like hearing about things I'd done, the places I went and what happened there, I often felt bad that he couldn't come along, that he was always stuck at home in his wheelchair. I had to think about how to tell the story so it felt like we were sharing something and not that I was oblivious to his situation. I would give him the pennant and I would keep the small baseball bat that was a ballpoint pen.

"Now I know what they mean when they say it's a nice place to visit but I wouldn't want to live there," my father said. His window was down and the little vent, the wing window, was open in such a way that he could flick the ash off his cigar by poking it out there. I thought that was pretty cool. "I mean, all those people on top of one another! How the hell do you figure out who to hate?" The player in the front passenger seat laughed, along with the two guys in back with me. "No. I'm serious!" my father went on. "How does a person know where he stands? I mean, people should get along, don't get me wrong. I just mean that when push comes to shove you have to know who you're for and who you're against, don't you?"

I've puzzled over that for a long time. The idea that *when* push comes to shove—not *if* push comes to shove—one must decide who one is for and against seems to have been the experience of many German Americans during the first half of the twentieth century. According to historian Daniel Okrent, in his *Last Call: The Rise and Fall of Prohibition*,

> Iowa declared speaking German in public or on the telephone unlawful. German books were burned in Wisconsin, playing Beethoven in public was banned in Boston, and throughout the country foodstuffs and street names of German origin were denatured

by benign Anglo-Saxonisms. Nearly ninety years before french fries became freedom fries during the Iraq War, sauerkraut became liberty cabbage and, in an odd homage to the president, Cincinnati's Berlin Street became Woodrow Street. "Cotton Tom" Heflin of Alabama, who could always be counted on to transcend the limits of ordinary, everyday bias, said, "We must execute the Huns within our gates. The firing squad is the only solution for these perverts and renegades."

Okrent goes on to quote from David M. Kennedy's account of the lynching of a German man in St. Louis and the court that found his murderers innocent.

Perhaps because my grandfather fought for the United States in the First World War, there was little question in the Hoffman house that his sons would fight in the Second. Don, Edgar, Francis, and Richard all served at the same time. This assumption was not unanimous among German Americans in Pennsylvania. Other families, other communities remained, in both wars, understandably divided, if not in their loyalties, then at least in their affections. It was important therefore to know, and prove, "who you're for and who you're against."

"My attitudes are my attitudes. They don't hurt nobody," my father insisted. Implicit in that statement was my father's understanding that he was inconsequential, powerless, and therefore free to hold whatever ideas he found comfortable, no matter their provenance, validity, or potential impact. His racism didn't matter so long as he treated individual people of color with respect. His misogyny didn't matter so long as he was not abusive to women. He hated the French whom he'd experienced during the war ("No self-respect," he judged of them), but had he met someone from France, I'm sure he would have been welcoming.

My father was born and died at Sacred Heart Hospital. He was baptized, confirmed, and married at Sacred Heart Church. He went to Sacred Heart School. In those days the parish was comprised of Irish, Italian, and German families with their attendant social clubs: the Hibernian club, St. Anthony's Association, Liederkranz. They were the Micks, the Dagos, and the Krauts, all innocent enough to my innocent ears: Micks were called that because their last names began with Mc. Dagos I couldn't figure, so I settled for inversion: since my father called spaghetti sauce "Dago sauce," I figured that Italians were Dagos because they ate a lot of spaghetti, which I knew to be true, so that must be it. And Krauts likewise. We were German, after all, and we ate a lot of sauerkraut, happily. No harm, no foul, as we said on the playground.

I do not mean to suggest that it was an innocent time. It was more likely an ignorant time, but when you're eight or nine years old, one often passes for the other. Things make sense in their own cockeyed way, shaped by the need to find the world benevolent or at least not poisonous. Later, as teens, maybe kick-started by hormones and disappointments, the whole view shifts, and every evidence of adult ignorance is taken for malice, every limitation of the adult world and the grown-ups in it seems willful, plotted, designed to deny us the fulfillment of our aspirations. An adult now, in need of more than a little understanding myself, I'm no longer so quick to condemn.

About the time he took a job laying railroad track for Bethlehem Steel, my father switched from cigars to cigarettes, which I suppose were easier to smoke on a short break from work. Outside in the cold you could put down your sledge, look down the track you'd laid, peel off your work gloves, shake out a Lucky, offer the pack around to the other guys, then spin the toothed wheel of your lighter, take that first drag, and exhale with something like a sigh.

My father was a smoke ring virtuoso. In the evening, at home, he entertained us with smoke rings through smoke rings, shapes we convinced ourselves, my brother Bobby and I, were animals, cars, trees, things made of breath that quickly broke apart and were gone.

But by the time I left for college, for New York City, my father had taken up a pipe. By then he was working in the office of the Recreation Department, overseeing the many sports leagues sponsored by the city, scheduling ball fields, courts, umpires, and referees. A pipe seemed right for a man who sat behind a desk, the sleeves of his white shirt rolled, the square Windsor knot of his tie loosened and the top button of his collar undone. I'd taken to smoking a pipe myself now that I was a college man, reading demanding books and writing carefully incomprehensible poems. I think we both had tweed jackets with leather patches on the elbows.

It took me my freshman year to figure out I wasn't getting much social traction from my man-of-letters get-up. My classmates and friends seemed at home in bell-bottom jeans and serapes, tie-dyed T-shirts, cowboy boots, leather jackets with rawhide fringe. By the fall of 1968, my sophomore year, I had the rudiments of a new self in place: a beard that grew mostly on my neck, hair down to my shoulders, a pair of secondhand boots from Goodwill, and the green canvas military bag designed to carry rounds of ammunition. I had not been home that whole summer. I told my parents I'd found a job in New York, which was true, though not the reason I stayed away.

I am being kind to my younger self when I say that I was in the throes of a confusing transformation and could not withstand just then the reminders my family would be of the adolescent I was: the high school quarterback, the altar boy, the healthy son they didn't have to worry about. I was worried about myself: I was no longer who I'd been and not yet who I was becoming.

I felt that I couldn't climb from the cauldron where I was being transmuted into some new person I hardly knew. It would be like showing up with one hand a claw, the other a fin; one foot webbed and the other a cloven hoof. My plan was to "get my shit together" as we said back then, and present them with the man I had become. They would have to accept or reject that person, and I knew I wasn't him yet. I remember my mother's sigh on the phone—I can still hear it, along with her generous refusal to protest—when I told her I would not be coming home for the summer.

For whatever reason, whether I could not bear to go home and be "Dickie," whether I wanted to remain in the hashish-and-patchouli-scented new erotic freedom of the counterculture in Greenwich Village, or whether I preferred waiting tables to the pickax and shovel of the road crew job of the previous summer, I had abandoned her. I had abandoned all of them.

I was not returning to my role as emotional support for my mother; I would not be sitting at the kitchen table with her, drinking our cans of beer and filling a large cut-glass ashtray with the butts of our hope: new research into muscular dystrophy, the promise of chiropractic for slowing muscular degeneration, an article she'd read about "atomic" medicine, and swapping the off-color jokes, my mother's secret pleasure, that would lighten the mood for a moment.

I would not be helping my father lift my brothers Bob

and Mike from wheelchair to commode and back again, would not be part of the care schedule that required him to come home from work several times a day.

I would give up at last trying to sustain a meaningful friendship with Bobby, declining in his wheelchair, the un-selfconscious and once ferocious love we had for each other as boys eroded by his illness, by my relative health, my urgent youth.

My half-crazy youngest brother, Mikey, soothing himself with his continual drumming on the tray of his wheelchair, chanting nonsense syllables nonstop, rocking and banging his head, could become a comfortable memory I responded to with pity and affection.

And my brother Joe, five years my junior, could take up whatever slack I was leaving and I could assent with relief to his role in the family narrative as one who, like me, would be fine. *That boy is all right.*

And I would not have to return to a city where I breathed the shame and humiliation of boyhood rape. So long as I remained in New York, site of nearly infinite possibility for remaking myself, I could insist that what happened to me as a boy was of no consequence.

When I first arrived in New York, I lived in a board-inghouse in the Bronx. My roommate was a folksinger who played the banjo. Pete Seeger was his idol. Along with my tweed sport coat and khakis, I wore my hair in a flattop that I made stand up with a stick of wax in a retractable plastic container. Two of the other guys in the house had heard of a club downtown, at St. Mark's Place, called the Electric Circus. Did I want to come?

Patchouli, incense, a strobe light at once disorienting and requiring a heightened alertness for its visual interruptions, the place was full of bodies undulating in sync with the strange music—no banjos here!—and the light show was continually changing both the color and contour of the walls and ceiling. Tommy, Brian, and I stood against one wall as if we were at a high school dance. The only dancing I'd ever even almost done was at the Y on Friday nights at a "hop" run by the CYO where, as a varsity athlete, my role was to stand along the wall with a toothpick and with a serious look on my face that I never seemed to manage to get right.

So I took up my position against the pulsing wall as if I were some kind of lifeguard minding the swimmers on a day of tricky currents. I was smoking my meerschaum pipe. I found that I was especially watching one young woman who seemed to be in masquerade, a pirate at a costume party: silk scarves that accentuated her every move, bangles on her arms, big gold hoops hanging from her ears. When I say that I found myself watching her, I mean just that—I'd been watching her, mesmerized, a long time before I was at all conscious of it. Maybe it's more accurate to say that I *lost* myself watching her.

All I am sure of is that I was lost.

I pushed off from the wall and into the throbbing room, moving through the dancers. Soon I was behind her. She was dipping down into a deep shimmy and moving as if she were trying to scratch her ears with first one shoulder then the other. I touched her, gently, to get her attention.

"Wanna dance?" I shouted over the music.

Maybe if I hadn't been so disoriented by the whole scene I would have understood that when she said, "What?" she was not asking me to repeat the question louder. When I did, she said something I'd never heard from a woman's lips: "Fuck off, asshole!"

This was not the CYO. I wasn't sure what it was, but I wanted it. I wanted to know women who danced like that and were tough enough to flash that kind of rage. I wanted to grow my hair and swing it around like so many of these guys. I wanted to grow a beard. Mostly I wanted to understand what was going on because I had just discovered, my naiveté plundered by a pirate goddess, that I was deeply and dangerously bored. I was at the end of a chapter of my life and only now knew it, as if I had turned a page expecting more of the same and found it blank.

I headed back to Tommy and Brian, who were changing colors, disappearing and reappearing, and blinking in the strobe. "I gotta get outa here," I said. I would come back, that I was sure of, but right now I wanted to head back to my room and begin changing.

I visited my family in August.

The bus from Port Authority was late arriving in Allentown, and my father was parked at the curb, the motor running. What a shock I must have been to him with my pubic beard under my chin, my hair in a ponytail, my torn jeans and clunky boots. I opened the door and threw my ammo bag in the back seat. The frown on his face was all puzzlement and perplexity. He offered his hand. I grasped it with my right and reached with my left arm to surround him and pull him to me, and I kissed him on his scratchy cheek. His foot must have slipped from the brake to the gas and next thing we know—boom!—we've lurched forward into the bumper of a taxi idling in front of us. "Jesus Christ!" The cabbie, black, was at the window pointing and yelling, my father apologizing. When the cab driver continued, offering his opinion of my father's driving skills, I saw my father's face change. "All right, that's enough," he said, "get back in your cab!" as if he were giving an order. I saw the cabbie's face change, too. He huffed, flared his nostrils, shook his head slowly, but quickly returned to his cab.

"Goddamn it," my father said, backing up, shifting, pulling out. After a block or two he nodded toward the back seat. "So when did you start carrying a purse?"

By the time we got to the house on Thirteenth Street, my father had turned this into a funny story. "Did you see the look on his face? Poor nigger's just sitting there waiting for his next fare and—bam!—we're up his ass!" We were out of the car, my bag slung over my shoulder. He looked at me, smirked, and shook his head. "Wait till your mother gets a load of you. She's going to shit."

The white wooden balustrade of the front porch, which had been missing a few balusters, had been replaced by two sections of black wrought iron. The railing up the front steps was made of pipes. The floor of the porch was green indoor/outdoor carpet. Things were changing here, too, at home, as I still called it.

But even then, I knew that had I stayed I would have rotted in that house. That house of dying, of sorrow and anger, of violence and doomed love, of waiting, always, for death; that house of sighs and separate rooms and cases of beer and cartons of cigarettes, of phlegmy coughs and curses and apologies and the next day the same day, the same unchanging deadness, numbness all the pleasure one could expect, oblivion as relief and love reduced to duty, family ties reduced to staying the hell out of the way, becoming invisible, silent and reliable, no needs of your own, never mind desires. I never say that I left. I don't even say I got out. I say I got the hell out, I got the fuck out. I spit the words, defying the old guilt at leaving. I curse in order to touch once again for a brief moment the rage that propelled me the hell out of there, the fuck out of there, the selfish fury that afforded me a life.

&

I was teaching at a boarding school where I had learned, by observing not only the other "masters," but the students, how to pass for middle class, a matter of dress, carriage, kinds of mixed drinks, brands of imported beer. Half my wardrobe was from Goodwill, the other half from clothes that graduating seniors left behind. I was all becoming and striving, trying to bootstrap myself into something like middle-class respectability, play-acting the young schoolmaster. I was more certain who I was not: I was not the boy who had been raped, whose brothers had died, whose father had beat him, a boy made of coal and steel and violence and trucks and shame. I was not him.

I was again, or still, learning how to be, who to be, a project that required the refusal of who I was. I was a showman in the classroom, alternately dancing across the front of the room, filling the blackboard, whirling to call on someone, or giving an assignment and then leaning by an open window, smoking my pipe. And in the evening, after dinner, I sat in the big, black leather recliner my father gave me when he bought a new one to put in the spot by the window, sat there as if strapped in it, the heavy rocks glass half empty of Tennessee sour mash, filling myself with dread.

Kathi and I, in an attic apartment above a boys' dormitory, were as yet only precariously married, untested. One day I came back to the apartment during a free period. There was a note for me tacked to the doorjamb:

Gone to buy baby food. Love, Kathi

I shook with excitement, joy, fear. I let out a whoop, and then another, dancing and swirling in the living room. I was going to be a father! I poured myself a drink.

During Kathi's pregnancy, I found myself revisiting every notion I ever had about being a man, asking what was worthwhile to bequeath to our son, and what I ought to uproot and discard, questioning everything, wondering on some level if my father was as good a man as I had always believed. More to the point, I questioned if I was a good man, or if I could become one, and I even wondered, at one point, if I was really my father's son: how could I, with so many questions, be the son of a man who seemed to have none?

&

Veronica and I are having tea in the kitchen while D watches cartoons in the living room. I tell her I have been thinking about the long arc of my father's life. I have a photo of him as a child before a 1928 Ford Model A with a horse and cart also in the picture. I mention how glad I am that he got to meet his great grandson.

"That was awesome, Dad. There was so much love in that house that weekend. It was just awesome. And you know what? I don't care what you think. Wait, I don't mean it like that, I mean I don't *know* what you think, but I can't help it; I feel like Poppop's got my kid's back. You know? He's not going to let anything bad happen to him. This is his boy. Maybe you think this is stupid."

"No, no. Say more about that."

"It's like the way I know that Grandma Dolly has always looked out for me. I've always felt that. I always felt like she had my back."

She asks me if it is true that my mother taught my brother Joe to read by the time he was four. "Did she teach you, too?"

I find myself instantly flooded with emotion: grief and gratitude, affection and rage, regret and yearning. "Yes. Yes, she did."

It is a bitter irony that my mother is called Grandma Dolly—even by me, talking to either of my children—when this is in fact precisely who she never got to be. She would have doted on her grandchildren, especially on Veronica since over and over she had hoped for a girl. "But every damn time, they'd come with that little attachment," she'd say, shaking her head and grinning, sometimes crooking her pinky to suggest infantile maleness. Sometimes, when grief returns like this, not with tears or simple sorrow but with a metallic taste like blood in my mouth, I don't know whether I am grieving for my mother who never had the chance to know my children or for my children who only know her as a constellation of anecdotes, responses to their questions. No doubt, grieving on behalf of someone dead is a kind of sentimentality since the dead, I feel certain, experience no pangs of regret. But that my children did not have her love and humor, her support and guidance, I count as a tragedy. And I believe that their beauty, their innocence, and their need might well have saved her from a despair that fueled her addiction. When I think of my mother smoking upward of three packs a day of unfiltered Chesterfields, when I recall her lighting the next cigarette with the butt of the last, the heavy glass ashtrays overflowing all over the house, I see the link between the words despair and desperation.

My mother didn't believe in kindergarten; she felt that she could give us a better start if she worked with us at home. I don't recall learning to read, only that I already knew how when I went to school, but I do remember her teaching Joe. She read to him sitting on her lap, and when he took his fingers from his mouth, slapped the page, said something, and craned his neck to look up at her, she lavished her praises on him, repeating something like what he'd said, pointing to the object and then the word in the storybook spread out before them.

"Do you miss him?"

Steeped in my reverie of my mother, it takes me a moment to understand that we are still talking about my father. In this brief moment of confusion, I miss both of my parents acutely and also my brothers Bobby and Mike. It is like the Auden poem: "A crack in the teacup opens/ a lane to the land of the dead." I almost tell her this, but I don't trust my motive: I am a hair's breadth from self-pity, from remarking that most of my family is dead. "Sure, I miss him."

"Poppop always made me feel special," Veronica says, "and he's looking out for D. I can feel it."

I would be harder on my father than I am if I didn't know what he means to Veronica. His legacy is complex, problematical—but his granddaughter's view of him is also a part of it.

I'm back in Allentown for the first time since my father's death. It's very odd because my brother, while different from our father in his ways, looks like a younger version of him, and he is sitting in the big recliner by the window. "Oh, and one more thing," Joe says, "I'm trying to gather up things you might want to have. All those videotapes of your kids when they were little?"

"Oh yeah, I'd love to have those."

"Well, that's what I'm trying to tell you: you know there was a period of time when, well, you know how he was, when the old man was into watching pornography and he would record it from the cable late at night and, well, he recorded over those tapes, some. You'll be watching Robert or Veronica swimming or playing soccer, and then all of a sudden—Whoa! There's a big vagina or some guy's dick or, you know. So I'm trying to edit them. I know a guy who can edit out that stuff and put it all on a DVD for you."

My brother seems able to accept this more easily than I. Am I being a prude? I halfway wish he hadn't told me this. I have been trying in the short time since his death to settle on a version of my father, if not to make grieving simpler, then to have something to say when friends ask what he was like. The portrait I've managed is uncomfortably complex, and now I can see that not only is it not the truth, it's not even the truth about my memory of him. I don't know what my brother understands when he says, "Well, you know how he was," but he's right, I do know, and I have known for a long, long time.

I would have made a great burglar; I had the training. I remember, when I was first going through puberty and tormented by a hormonal urgency amplified by the sexual abuse of the preceding couple of years, I discovered my father's cache of "dirty magazines" on the floor in the corner of the bathroom closet. First, my hands shaking, I noticed everything I could about the stack. What item of clothing had been draped in front of the magazines to veil them and exactly how? Was there an edge that stuck out a bit when they were in the pile? Were any of the magazines in the stack reversed or upside down? It was necessary to keep them strictly in the order in which I'd found them, which required tremendous patience because my heart was racing with both erotic anticipation and fear. The best way to assure that I wouldn't be caught was to assume that my father would notice any small detail that had changed, or even that he had laid a trap for me. When I was through I had to remember and honor all my minute observations, leaving no trace of my trespass there.

What does it mean that there is an image I remember

from that time as clearly as I recall any of my teachers, my neighbors, my friends' sisters and mothers? The woman in the photo is not a "pinup," one of those posters of actresses printed for soldiers overseas. She is looking at the camera (at me!) with a beguiling half smile, bare breasted, and shielding her privates with a triangular pillow that she appears to be about to discard. I turn the page, but now she is lying on her belly and I still can't see. I am alert as a mouse in a cupboard. There is no lock on the bathroom door. What was that noise? Is somebody coming?

I was first introduced to pornography two years earlier by the coach who raped me and many, many other boys over a forty-year career. I understand pornography as an instrument of oppression. Certainly activists like Catharine MacKinnon and Andrea Dworkin and Susan Griffin make a sound case for the role of pornography in the maintenance of a strictly gendered status quo in which women are exploited. But what if my father, completely in thrall to these images for apparently his entire life, is understood instead as a kind of devotee, a poor man's Robert Graves, worshipping moon and *mons*, vulva, curve, and shadow? Can this view be squared with what was also, clearly, an addiction? I don't know. Could pornography be a vestige of paganism, like the sheela-na-gigs on the walls of Irish churches from the Middle Ages, images that remind the viewer of the power of female sexuality, including the power to call forth unquenchable desires, to stir seed, to wake passion?

In my lifetime I have seen women emerge from their domesticated status—as *pets*, which was literally the term for women who fit a certain standard of beauty a little darker than the girl-next-door "Playmate" image of Hugh Hefner's *Playboy*. In fact, *Playboy*, for the longest time, remained somewhat romantic, and its airbrushed models could be seen to be idealizations, all contour and softnesses and pouts and smiles. *Penthouse* "Pets" were the first big-money, mainstream offering of photographs designed to ignite the testosterone/adrenaline fuse, with the hair and sometimes sweat that *Playboy* excised. Mainly, however, there were vaginas. There were cunts, twats, beavers, honeypots, and quim. There were pussies and cut, koochies and boxes. The pornification of pop culture had begun: the cat was out of the bag; that is, the pussy was down off the top shelf and out of its plain brown wrapper. I think that we are still reeling from it, still in need of an ethics of sexuality that has less to do with body parts and more to do with power, less to do with secrecy, censorship, and shame, and more to do with how we treat one another.

Am I merely trying to rehabilitate my father by seeing him as a devout worshiper of the Goddess, albeit an inverted and benighted one? After all, certain images are so elemental, such basic emblems of the features of human life, that they transcend the meanings ascribed to them by their context, their culture, their era. What of those figures in coitus on Indian temples? What of those sheela-na-gigs? What was their function? They seem shocking and cartoonish and vulgar to us now, women hiking up their skirts, holding open their vaginas. Were they meant as a reminder of the prepatriarchal order of things? An insistence by converts that the protectress of the harvest be honored in the temple of the sky god?

When overcome by shame, I would pray to the holy mother, Our Lady, the Blessed Virgin, and desperately ask her to intercede in heaven on my behalf. I gravitated to her altar to the left of the sanctuary where, for all her gentle femininity, I was able, even encouraged, to pour out all my shame and ask for her help. What I wanted her to do was convince her son and his father, that patriarchal dyad, that I was not the vile thing I knew they would judge me to be, that I was penitent, sorry, salvageable.

To this day I wonder if I was sloppy, if I overlooked some tiny feature, or replaced one of the magazines upside down, or forgot to drape the bathrobe across the stack as it should have been. I suppose it could have been an accident, or my father operating on a hunch, but all at once he was there, pulling me up from where I crouched over a pouting woman offering me her breasts. He had easily a hundred pounds on me, and he threw me up against the wall with hardly any effort, his hand on my throat. Still unzipped, I was trying to cover myself.

"I got you, you little sneak. What is it you think you're doing? Huh? I ought to drag you downstairs right now, just like this," he looked down where I'd covered my shame with my hands, "and show your mother what her darling boy's been up to." I was shaking my head from side to side, pleading—not my mother! He let go. "Put those away now and get yourself together. What if your mother had walked in on you doing that?"

I fell to my knees, face burning and ashamed, put the pile of magazines together, and slid them deep into the dark of the closet. As I crawled back out, I heard my mother. "What's going on up there?"

My father glared at me with a strange expression, no longer anger; something *like* anger, but different, as if taking my measure, deciding that although I was a disappointment I would have to do. Without taking his eyes from mine, he answered her. "Nothing. Nothing to worry about." He nodded toward the bathroom door and as I walked through it he put his hand on my shoulder. Then he swiveled past me and went swiftly down the stairs and out the front door with not another word.

It never occurred to me to wonder if my mother knew about my father's magazines. I wonder at that now. She must have known about them. What did she make of them? I suspect she thought of them as merely naughty, a word she used to describe the off-color jokes she enjoyed. And I didn't understand, at age twelve, how my father had managed, putting his hand on my throat, to convince me to carry the shame for both of us on that occasion. Maybe that's what his measuring gaze had been about; maybe he'd decided that, still halfway a child and thus inadequate, I was nonetheless capable of carrying his shame. All I thought about, watching from the window as he walked down the street with his hands in his pockets, was how long before it was safe to revisit my father's paper harem.

I have been teaching writers for nearly twenty years, focused especially on the memoir and the personal essay. I don't believe it's an accident that the memoir, a genre earlier mainly the province of the well born and those with heroic or salacious tales to tell, became one of the chief ways to talk back to the worldview in which the postwar boomer generation was indoctrinated. You need money to make a movie and your stories need to make money on television. A memoirist, an essayist, needs only his or her skill as a writer and a commitment to pursue the truth.

Among the many stories of coming of age are stories of coming out, of rape, of war, of atrocity, and betrayal. I feel privileged, if sometimes exhausted, to be afforded this view of history pouring through the narrow sluice of an individual life. One of the stories I have read again and again, its particulars changing but its basic situation the same, is the younger sister's story. It goes, roughly, like this: older brother, twelve or thirteen, has found his father's cache of pornography, and after masturbating to the films whenever no one else is home, one day decides to try what he's seen there with his younger sister. After all, the women seem to enjoy it, too, moaning with pleasure and desire. So he crawls into his sister's bed. She is nine or ten. At first they giggle together at what he is telling her, at what he is showing her. She trusts him, after all. They're playing. And then they are not. And then she wants him to stop and he won't. And then she wants him to stop coming to her bed and he won't. And she won't tell, cannot tell. For years. Until now. In some, the story ends with the whole family aligned against the daughter. In others, she must never tell— even though she has been unable to have a trusting, intimate relationship, ever—because it would destroy not only her brother and her parents (whom she half believes already know) but her sister-in-law and her beloved nieces and nephews.

Who is to blame in this story? Who is responsible for how many times this story is repeated?

I remember vividly, viscerally, the power of the feelings—chemicals, really, as surely as any drug—that tore through me as a pubescent boy encountering pornography and how easy it must have been for the coach whose color slides exploited that arousal. And then, of course, there were my father's magazines. There were no videotapes in those days. I had no sisters.

Is anyone in the story spared? What is the cost to the ones who know? To those who do not? To those who know but insist they do not? We live, it seems, mostly on a need-to-not-know basis. Our chief defense is belief in a place called elsewhere, a place where our children and grandchildren will never live.

&

In the days before Kathi's surgery in early September, just a few weeks after my father died, we were once again renegotiating our intimacy. I would not have said so at the time, but now I don't know how else to describe those conversations. She didn't want me to come with her, insisting there was no need and asking only that I be available by phone so she could call me to pick her up. I wanted to wait downstairs in the hospital cafeteria, close by, in case anything went wrong.

"You just want to get out of that first faculty meeting," she said. It was a good-humored reference to our frustration with academic bureaucracy, but I mistook it for an accusation of selfishness. Instead of responding the way Kathi had expected, I pouted. It was as if she had spoken from within our history, our shared understandings, but I had responded from outside of that intimacy. Maybe because I was still mourning my father, I was more his son than Kathi's husband just then. Maybe I was already so full of self-accusation and guilt that I expected to be chastised.

Things were changing. Robert was getting on his feet. He had found a job and moved into a place of his own nearby. Veronica had begun her career as a nurse. D was in daycare. Damion was in jail. A new semester was about to begin, and though I am usually excited to meet my new students, I was feeling only drained and tired. I felt as if Kathi was holding me at arm's length when all she wanted was to keep things as normal as possible. I complied with her wish, and when I got the phone call I picked her up and brought her home, where Veronica was cooking something on the stove and

D was in his highchair smearing slices of banana around on his tray and eating dry Cheerios.

Three weeks later we got the news that Kathi needed another surgery. The oncologist reassured her that the cancer was not invasive; however, the surgeon had not gotten "clear margins" around the cancer they removed. A second surgery in this case had only a 60 percent rate of success. If the second surgery failed, the alternative would be a mastectomy, followed by chemotherapy and radiation.

&

I'm driving west on Route 2 to Concord to visit Damion, and I am thinking hard about how things have turned out so far. I have questions about what I don't know and feelings I don't understand. I'm still trying to piece together what I know about the chain of events that leads to our meeting behind the brick wall that rises on my left as I circle the rotary and pull into the parking lot. I turn off the car and stare at the tower in the near corner of the enclosure and the coils of razor wire atop the chain-link around the perimeter. Cameras and floodlights are aimed at this green space between the wall and the fence. A camera also takes in the parking lot.

I'm about to get out of the car; I have my hand on the door handle when I see an army of dark-blue uniforms coming toward the parking lot. I have arrived as the shift is changing, a mistake. I stay in the car. In truth, I feel intimidated. I do not want to be the single ununiformed male body moving toward the prison against this tide.

I bear some responsibility, not blame, for Damion's incarceration. I was trying to help. I watched him and Veronica in those first weeks after the baby was born as they laughed, argued, sulked, made up, laughed some more, and

I thought that I would do anything to keep such joy from being snatched away. It seemed to me that they were actually creating the world we had only been able to wish for. One day, buoyed by their love and laughter, I made a slideshow of all the photos I'd taken of them since the baby was born. I gave it a good Jamaican soundtrack: Bob Marley. "Three Little Birds" ("Don't worry/ 'bout a t'ing/cause every little t'ing/ gonna be all right") and "No Woman No Cry." We danced around the living room laughing, handing the baby around from one to another.

With Damion coming up for trial, I wrote to the DA. I thought it was a masterful piece of rhetoric, and I didn't see how he could not agree with me:

12 OCTOBER 2007

Dear District Attorney Leone:

I'm writing to implore you to personally intervene in the case of Damion Smith, now scheduled to be tried in Cambridge District Court on October 24th. I am writing as the father of Damion's girlfriend, and the grandfather of his son, born in early August. Obviously I have an interest in Damion's remaining out of jail, for my daughter's sake, her baby's, and Damion's as well. I also think I can offer some perspective on this young man and his situation.

Damion has won me over during the past year or so. No doubt you can imagine my initial skepticism, indeed my resistance. I did not know Damion when my daughter, a junior in the Boston College nursing program, announced that she was pregnant. Perhaps understandably, I was extremely wary of him. Since then, however, I have had occasion to

spend time with him on nearly a daily basis, and
I see him as a young man who drifted off course
and suffered near disastrous consequences. As you
are doubtless aware, Damion has served time in
federal prison for an offense that occurred during
the same very short time period as that for which
he is now charged.

During that short time period, Damion was
trying to make enough money to return to school.
He was studying business and wanted to obtain his
contractor's license. He had completed one year of a
two year community college program, but he ran out
of money, and like a lot of young men succumbed to
the allure of some quick cash.

Since his release, Damion has been trying
to make things somehow come out right. I am
impressed with his sensitivity, his thoughtfulness,
his warmth and sense of humor. He is a doting
father and a committed, deeply loving partner to my
daughter. He has become a member of our family,
and I am willing to help him in any way I can.

Like many other young men I encounter (my son
is twenty-three, and I teach at Emerson College,)
Damion sometimes seems a little lost in dealing with
the complex realities of today's world and fitting into
it, and he needs mentoring, coaching, and advice. I
am convinced that he sees a different path opening
up for him now, and although he knows that it will
not be easy (already he has encountered the trouble
finding work that a CORI check, not to mention an
open case, almost ensures,) he is committed to never
repeating his past mistakes. More than that, he has
embraced fatherhood with real joy and a genuine

commitment to be an active, loving father to his infant son. He walks the floors with him at night, he feeds him from a bottle so my daughter can study, he reads to him, sings to him, changes his diapers, soothes him. It is a joy for me, as a grandfather, to see. He has taken the initiative to become a member of the Carpenter's Union Apprenticeship Program, and he is actively visiting work sites, speaking with shop stewards and supervisors, looking for his opportunity.

Damion is a young man who exercised decidedly bad judgment, paid the consequences, and has grown up a great deal since the offense for which he is now charged. That offense took place before his incarceration in the Federal system. Upon his release, those charges, which had been *nol prossed*, were reinstated. I do not know why, but I suspect that the purpose was to ensure public safety since, after all, the charges included gun possession. However, this young man, who has made his time in prison into exactly what we all hope for, and has demonstrated his willingness, his eagerness, to transform himself, is no threat to public safety.

Please allow me to put my remarks here in a broader context. I have been a victim advocate for more than a decade now, since the publication of my first book led to the arrest of a serial child molester. I have been and continue to be outspoken about violence against women and children and the brutalizing effects of the socialization of boys. Until recently I served on the steering committee of the Governor's Commission on Sexual and Domestic Violence, and I am a member of the Men's Initiative for Jane Doe.

I have been nominated for the Boston Area Rape Crisis Center's Champion of Change award. I have keynoted Attorney Generals' conferences in Massachusetts, New Hampshire, and Vermont. I mention these things so you will understand that I take issues of crime and safety extremely seriously.

That said, I cannot see how anyone is served by incarcerating this young man for something he did nearly three years ago, in what was truly a former life. There are no victims, yet, in this case; no one is crying out for redress. This is an old offense that harmed no one. I cannot see how taking a newborn's father from him will further anything resembling justice, and I expect that, in addition to creating victims where there are none, it would make of this young man of renewed promise an utterly discouraged person. He has been doing everything he possibly can to demonstrate that he is no longer the young man who exercised such poor judgment two and a half years ago. Please, I am begging you, do not allow this young person's efforts to be for nothing; please do not allow him to be thrown away.

One year from now the Commonwealth could be home to a new household of productive taxpaying parents, headed by a union carpenter and a registered nurse. Or the Commonwealth could break up a young family, separate a parent and child, and incur the considerable expense of incarcerating a young man who, under some financial duress, made a wrong turn nearly three years ago.

You will receive letters from other members of my

family as well. We are asking that mandatory minimum sentences not be sought in Damion's case. I can
assure that you would never regret such an action.
Damion has been in complete compliance with
supervision after his time in prison (I have spoken
to his Federal Probation Officer who thinks highly
of him) and we are asking that the Commonwealth
be satisfied to place him under stringent supervision
for a length of time that would allow him to demonstrate that he is a contributing, law-abiding citizen.

Should you have any wish to talk further about
this matter, please don't hesitate to call me.

Richard Hoffman

The guards are pouring toward me, taking their car keys
from their pockets, calling out to one another, looking tired
and glad their shift is over, just like workers leaving an auto
plant or a steel mill. I am reflecting, with growing anxiety,
on what, driving here, I have been coming to understand
as the part I played in the way events unfolded. The story I
have been telling myself, of the magnanimous and wronged
Samaritan, has begun to unravel.

A guard knocks on my window, startling me. I fumble
a moment, panicky, put my key back in the ignition, and
turn the car on to lower the window. He points across my
windshield, "Just a reminder. Your inspection expires this
month."

"Thanks. Thanks a lot." I'm trying to decide if he's being friendly or officious. Then he smiles. "Mine ran out last
month. I weren't paying attention and got a ticket. Okay.
Take care!"

"You, too. Thanks."

&

Not too long after I sent that letter, Damion and Veronica began fighting. At first we thought it was just the pressure of living with us in the crowded house we were all finding stressful. Kathi and I both tried to assure them we understood, having lived with Kathi's parents for a year. But there were other things going on, just as there were when we lived with Kathi's parents. One fight had to do with the image of a naked woman Veronica glimpsed on Damion's cell phone. She found it insulting; he felt he had a right to it. I thought about all I would risk as a boy for another glimpse of the goddess of the triangular pillow. What seems clear to me was that Damion was feeling trapped by the routine, caged by the tight space, awkwardly trying to live in someone else's household, and chafing at his lack of access to other friends. For a young man, probably even more so for one who has been to prison, being incarcerated with loved ones is still being incarcerated. And, of course, hanging over him always was the prospect of returning to prison. How could he afford to give Veronica his heart under such circumstances? And how could she fully give hers? They both loved their infant son; no protecting oneself from the pain of that attachment.

Damion started going out evenings, coming home late. One night in early December, Damion came down the stairs and put on his coat. Before I could greet him he turned and went out. Veronica followed close behind. "Daddy, talk to him. He listens to you!" I put on my coat, caught up with him at the end of the block. It was the coldest night so far that winter. "You want company?" I asked him. I don't know what I would have said next if he'd said no. He shrugged. "Yeah. Sure." We walked. I didn't ask where we were going; we just walked the avenue. I tried to convey that I understood, although I didn't, only thought I did. I talked to him about postpartum, about how hard it can be for a woman in the weeks and months after giving birth. Besides being a mother, Veronica was working part time and going to school full time. It put a lot of responsibility on Damion. I said we understood this and that we admired him for it. I said I understood what it's like to be a new father living in a household in which you have no standing, where nothing is yours, and you have no say in even simple daily decisions. I promised him things would get better. I hugged him. "Don't walk away from this," I said. "You can make this work. Don't walk away."

"I have to think."

"Well, I'm going back. I'm freezing my ass off out here. You coming?"

"I have to think. You go ahead."

He came back hours later, in the dead of night; he was there to take over his shift with the baby in the morning when Veronica left for school.

By Christmas he was no longer living with us. The official story was that he and Veronica were trying to sort things out while Damion lived with his aunt. In fact, it seems now that he had a number of places he could sleep, none of them alone. He continued to work out child-care arrangements with Veronica so she could study.

One night Damion came to the house to bring back baby D and Veronica saw a young woman sitting in the passenger seat of his car, playing with the baby, tickling him. She roared down the stairs and let him feel the fullness of her rage at his betrayal. "He's my son! He is not for you to show off to your girlfriends! He's my son! He's not a puppy!" The baby was wailing. Kathi, Robert, and I were all there in the small front hallway. Veronica continued to rage at him.

"She's not my girlfriend," Damion kept saying. "Veronica, you've got this all wrong." But it didn't matter to her who the woman in the car was; she knew, and it twisted her guts to know, that there were other women. She took the baby upstairs, soothing him.

Damion looked around at us, his expression saying, "See? How can I reason with her when she's like this?" He sighed and shook his head. "She's not my girlfriend. She's my cousin."

When no one spoke, he left.

All through this time, we continued our efforts to convince the DA to drop the old charges, or at least make a deal that did not include returning to prison. I spoke to our state representative, and I wrote to the governor with whom I had recently shared the dais at a White Ribbon Day event opposing domestic violence. A friend who knew the DA personally agreed to pay him a visit and talk with him about the case.

The weeks and months passed and nothing seemed to be working. I decided to write an op-ed. I had been published in the opinion pages of the *Boston Globe* twice before, and I was serving on the board of a nonprofit with one of its former editors, so I felt I might have some access. It all seemed to me to be about access. Because Damion was politically inconsequential, he was disposable, like hundreds of thousands of poor and working-class people, especially young black men.

Rereading the piece I sent to the paper, I see that it was more than an appeal; I was attempting to shame the DA into changing his mind. I didn't allow myself to see this at the time. I was convinced I had the moral high ground and that the tone of the piece was right.

I wrote that a grave injustice was about to be done in

the name of justice, that an old and victimless crime was about to claim its first victim, a six-month-old baby boy who would be separated from his father. "He is, after all, a black boy. Maybe he needs to get used to it, prison, as a feature of his life. Statistics suggest this is so. But neither he nor his father are statistics, they are the latest victims of institution-alized racism. If this trial occurs, this costly and senseless prosecution, then our judicial bureaucracy is even more out of control than anyone thought."

Instead, and wisely, the *Globe* gave the story to one of its columnists, Adrian Walker, who met with Damion and me. I'd shown Damion the piece I wrote. He didn't like it, didn't like seeing himself as a victim.

Another friend of mine put me in touch with the best defense attorney in Massachusetts, who agreed, as a favor to our mutual friend, to work for half his usual retainer. Even this reduced fee was a hardship for us, and Kathi was angry that she was not consulted. Things felt to me that they were moving and moving fast, and the fact that I did not slow them down long enough to confer with her was a mistake, not only because that was our agreement about spending any large sums of money, but because something had be-gun to creep back into my behavior that I should have seen and understood. It is true that I wanted Veronica and Da-mion to have a decent chance to make a family, but it was also true that I was getting caught up in the battle, sending e-mails, making phone calls, meeting with the defense at-torney, talking to anyone who might have any leverage. I had decided it was a matter of principle: Damion would have all the advocacy a middle-class, well-connected white kid would have. But it was also, although I mostly hid this from myself, my exercising whatever social and political muscles I had built up by virtue of crossing the class line, of "moving up." It was my need to prove I was just as good as them. As I said, other things had kicked in, including the old male mythology about battling injustice on behalf of the underdog.

Walker's column ran the following Tuesday. It was strong but more politic than mine. A couple of days later, the district attorney responded with a letter to the editorial page. He took issue with the way Walker had framed the case and restated the charges in such a way that they suggested Damion was incorrigible.

District attorneys never, ever write letters to newspapers. They prefer to do their arguing in court, not in the media. I thought this was evidence of progress. It meant we were getting to him. I failed to see, even then, that I had changed the game from a considered appeal to his sense of fair play to a public assault on his integrity. I was too full of myself, wedded to the myth, to understand that by hiring the DA's arch nemesis, bringing pressure to bear from the statehouse, the governor's office, and the media (I had spoken to reporters at three TV stations, as well), I had not only changed the tone, I had challenged him, I had called him out. I believed I had outgrown this kind of aggressive taunting, and that I had only the welfare of my family at heart. Who could blame me? I was the good guy.

I was the fool. I was so certain I was right that, whether or not I was right, I was wrong. I had been giving myself a free pass, a vacation from self-examination, beginning even before I hired the defense attorney without consulting Kathi. When Veronica and Damion and D were living together in their own house, a family, without the threat of incarceration or, worse, the separation of a prison sentence, everyone would agree it had all been worth it. People might even remark how I had risen to the occasion, found, gathered, and deployed resources like a field general, and won one for the little guy. I would demur: "What else could I do?" As I said, a fool. I want to insist that I was a well-intentioned fool, but what other kind is there? An ill-intentioned fool is no fool at all but a villain.

Soon after that, the defense attorney informed me that the trial had been moved forward to May. He insisted that he hadn't done this so that I would have more time to agitate on Damion's behalf. He repeated this twice on the phone, and I took it as a wink and a nudge. The crusade continued.

Then one night, at the kitchen table, the baby asleep upstairs, Veronica told us something she had withheld from us for months, that Damion kept a handgun in the glove box of his car. She'd kept this information from us probably because the potential cascade from this revelation could destroy what was left of her dream of making a family. Love blinds us to good sense, but that night she was angry enough not to care.

"So he's driving around with the baby in the car seat and a loaded gun in the glove box? That's outrageous!" Kathi said. She was the one who, later, came up with the sensible and respectful idea that Damion could visit D here, or we would bring D to his mother's house, but under no circumstances could he be allowed to take the child anywhere on his own.

The next evening Damion came by to pick up D. As I heard his key in the front door, Veronica shouted down the stairs, "Don't you let him in here! Tell him to go away! I don't want him here!" She'd been upstairs crying, Kathi comforting her.

As the door opened, I blocked his entry. He looked up, surprised. "What's up?"

"She doesn't want to see you."

"Yeah. I know." He held up his cell phone. "She's mad. I just come by to get D."

Robert had turned off the TV and taken up a position behind me with his arms crossed.

"That's not going to happen," I said.

"I don't understand. What's going on here?"

"What's going on is you driving around with my grandson in the back of your car and a gun in the front, that's what's going on. And that is not happening again, ever."

Veronica and Kathi came halfway down and sat on the stairs, Veronica nursing the baby. Damion could see all of us now, aligned against him. He raised his hands in front of him, palms out, fingers spread, as if to say, "Whoa. Hold on a minute." I would rather not have seen the look in his tearing eyes then, and I hope to never have to see it again.

"Can we talk about this? Sit down and talk about it?"

"No. There's nothing to talk about."

"I don't understand."

"Go," I said. "You're no longer welcome here."

That afternoon I had e-mailed the defense attorney and told him we would no longer pay for him to represent Damion. I had written that I no longer believed that he had been truthful with us, and that I believed he had lied to us about a number of things, including having a gun in our house. I told him about the gun in the glove box.

Damion looked past me, and Robert behind me, to Veronica on the stairs. "How do I fix this? Veronica? I'm sorry. How do I fix this?"

"You can't. You can't fix it. You broke it."

"Wait. You get mad at me and now you want to throw me under the bus? I see. I see how it is." He turned to me, nodded to Kathi. "I got nothing but respect for you and Kathi. And Rob. You're the closest thing I've had to a real family. I don't know what to do right now."

"Right now? Right now you can go." I felt no satisfaction

saying it, and I hoped that Damion heard both meanings of *right now:* that he should go immediately, and that this was what he should do right now but, perhaps, not later. Maybe we all needed time to think.

Damion's mother agreed that Damion should visit D only at our house or hers. That plan was in place until a few weeks later on a Friday morning, the day before Veronica's baccalaureate assembly, when Damion went to the lawyer's office to meet about his trial, set for Monday. The attorney told him, "We're all done here. I suggest you go home, pack your bags, and make your good-byes. You're going away." He had worked out a plea with the prosecutor. Damion was to spend a year in the Middlesex House of Correction.

That same afternoon, Veronica called me at my office. "Daddy, he's scaring me. He says he's coming to get his son. He says I can't keep his son away from him."

I told her to go to a friend's house, and I went home to wait for Damion, hoping I'd be able to calm him down. He never showed up.

That night he was arrested with three friends and charged, again, with possession of drugs and firearms.

Now, on this visit, pulling myself together in the parking lot as the last of the guards are starting their cars and heading home, what I really want from Damion is the story of that evening. I have heard a number of accounts, all secondhand. I want to hear his recollections of that evening.

As I enter the building I notice for the first time that there are marked parking spaces just outside the door. One says Warden. One says State Police Commander. One says District Attorney. The ascending chain of command. I have never seen it more clearly: I had tried to help, but I made things worse.

&

Sometimes, if I'm talking with friends about our families or grandkids, I'll take out my phone with the photos of my grandson. If the friends are white, they stare a moment, say how beautiful he is, and then remark, "Ah, he's biracial." If they are friends of color, they say, "Oh, your grandson's black." I once asked about this and a friend I would have called biracial set me straight from his perspective: my grandson's black because history has defined him as such, because the white world will call him black, because he can only understand who he is in the eyes of the world by being black and because, alas, the police will call him black. I wonder if my friends who call him beautiful will still think so in a dozen years or if they will see him as dangerous until he can prove otherwise.

At any rate, often, after questions of proximity ("You're so lucky! My grandchildren are on the other coast!") and grade in school, white friends will ask, "Is the father still in the picture?" It is a strange, strained, locution. "The father"—not *his* father, or *the child's* or *the boy's* father, but *the* father, an abstraction, and I already sniff a bit of moralizing in the air. I don't try to dodge what's next; I say it: "Yes. But things are hard right now because the boy's father, Damion, is in prison."

The questions stop. No one asks why or what for. And I believe I know what they think because it is not really their thought, or mine—although I can almost reach out and touch it in the air between us—as much as it is a page from the American book of class and caste. It is as if a column of integers has been added, tallied, totaled, summed up: white trash. I don't want to own the thought, and I don't require anyone else to own it. I only wish that in these situations we could acknowledge the psycho/social/political chord that has just been played, that I hear as it fades, diminuendo, into a generalized discomfort as I put my phone back in my pocket. Would that this chord would fade into history as well.

It doesn't seem likely. Recently Veronica told me that when she was six or seven months pregnant, she visited the welfare office to see if she qualified for food stamps or any other assistance. The woman who took down her information asked her how much education she had. "Junior year in college." The woman gave her a condescending look and asked again.

"I've finished my junior year in college."

"No, dear. That's high school. You mean you finished your junior year in high school."

Veronica stood and left without signing up. White trash is not so much a group of people as the name of the category she, my beautiful and shamed daughter, felt she'd been consigned to as the hot tears welled in her eyes, her cheeks burned, and she gathered her things and left that office.

It's a slur. I don't allow my writing students to use the term. When I come upon it in a manuscript we're discussing, I call out the author: what do you mean? "You know," they say. But it turns out that they mean poor people, as we already knew. I try to ask my follow-up questions gently, without betraying my anger: do you mean my mother working in the sweater factory? My father laid off again? Are you talking about my aunt waitressing at the Uptown Diner? My next-door neighbor's mother working the Woolworth's lunch counter? Are you referring to my mother's stinky shoes she cut holes in to ease her corns while she worked on her feet eight hours a day? Or my father's brogans with the eye-sized hole in the bottom he patched by cutting a piece of linoleum for an insole?

They mean the people I grew up with, who lived in "the wards," in the lower street numbers, near the river and the slaughterhouse and the breweries, in neighborhoods with few detached houses and dogs that were not for petting but protection. They mean my cousin Joanne, "gone to live with the coloreds." They mean all those who have not ascended the class ladder, who either failed or never tried in the first place, perhaps for very good reasons the students would not understand.

They mean, it has turned out again and again, these students of mine, they mean the people they are leaving behind, distanced by ridicule, the people who raised them.

White trash is a term related historically to the establishment of race as a political designation and justification for atrocity. In his two-volume work, *The Invention of the White Race,* historian Theodore Allen traces the origins of the American class/race dynamic to 1676 Chesapeake, in the Virginia Colony that Allen calls "our society's first living cell," the site of what came to be known as Bacon's Rebellion, an uprising that threatened to overthrow an agricultural system in which 5 percent of the planters owned the land and therefore the labor of all who lived on it, no matter what continent they had come from. Allen says that the significance of that uprising is that "a century and a half before Nat Turner led his rebellion, and William Lloyd Garrison began the *Liberator,* the armed laboring class, black and white side by side, fought for the abolition of slavery."

In the decades that followed, laws were enacted that meted out certain small privileges to those from Europe to ensure their loyalty. So-called "miscegenation" was criminalized, as were nearly all easy relations between European, African, and native groups of the laboring class. These laws came to govern the entire plantation system on which the nation was built. Once these laws became established, the traffic in Africans became easier to justify. What's more, they served as the template for the legal framework of apartheid in South Africa and Hitler's Nuremberg Laws concerning "racial purity."

I am only recounting what I have learned, what is easily available to all who want to know, in order to make my point here: the air, the atmosphere of a conversation about my grandson, about his parents, his future, is tainted still, poisoned by the particulate of history, of the crime of trading in human flesh, human labor, human lives.

I asked a friend of mine once how I, a white man, ought best to deal with this history now, in my own life. An African American poet and professor, one who has given a great deal of thought to all this, he replied, "Try not to be an asshole."

But white trash or not, what class am I? And how has that played out in the lives of my children?

"I think it was my hair," Veronica says. We've been looking at a folder of D's preschool homework, sitting at the kitchen table; I had asked her why she never hung around with the white kids growing up. "It probably sounds really stupid but I think it was my hair. Everybody just assumed I was mixed. They didn't see me as a white girl with this kinky hair. And Alyssa was my best friend." Alyssa's parents are African American and Japanese American.

"So you felt more comfortable with friends of color?"

"Well, it wasn't like I fit in with the white kids! I wasn't coming back from school vacations in Aruba or the south of France."

"Yeah, but they probably never got to go to Allentown." I made a face at her.

Must I say how sad this conversation made me? How

close to despair it brings me to think that we are all required to live in this continuing absurdist tragedy where race and class intersect?

And what about this ache that I keep pushing away, this need to know if my daughter, in always choosing black boyfriends, is rejecting me? I am ashamed of this concern. I understand how elementally racist it is, and I resist it and feel angry at myself for my inability to escape my upbringing. The ghost of my Uncle Francis? Did he feel rejected by my cousin Joanne? Spurned and defied without the benefit I've had of all that's changed since then, without the education I've received, without the habit—a luxury, really—of weighing and wondering at the way things are?

We have not come very far.

&

In more than twenty-five years of AA meetings, I have never heard a better description of the alcoholic's predicament than I heard from my son, Robert, in his first shaky weeks of abstinence, trying not only not to drink but to understand how he had gotten so lost in the first place.

"I'd start drinking with my friends and after a couple of drinks I could see how loose and easy everyone was. Everyone but me. So I had another, and then another. But I could never get there where everybody else seemed to be. I'd keep trying, but I always ended up passed out someplace. I'd wake up and wonder: what the fuck?"

It was my own experience when I was his age. My companions always seemed to be "lit"; their pleasure in one another, or the music, or the activity, was enhanced by a few drinks. I couldn't seem to get the light to go on, but I could see it flickering: if only I would try a little harder, have just one more.

But before long, it was precisely that unconsciousness I was seeking. By the time Robert was born, I was a solitary drinker. I had a satchel of papers to grade every night, and I would hole up in my study, in my father's old recliner, a rocks glass and a bottle next to me on the table, inching my way to oblivion as I corrected my high school students' grammar and usage and penciled occasionally legible comments in the margins. In the summers, and on school vacations, I was "working on my novel" in that same black hand-me-down chair.

I used to drive past a liquor store on the way home from the school where I was teaching. I would have finished the bottle of bourbon the night before—or worse, I would have fallen asleep with only an inch or two left in the bottom of the bottle, and I'd be behind the wheel, talking to myself. If I hit the red light at that corner, I would glare at the neon signs in the windows, jaw set, breathing hard through flared nostrils. You're not going to get me this time! I would tell myself that if I made it past the store without pulling into the parking lot, then I wasn't an alcoholic. After all, I was going home to a house where there was no alcohol. An alcoholic wouldn't do that! An alcoholic would be sure to have a bottle at the ready, maybe even a backup. A great relief washed over me as the light changed and I passed the store and soon after turned onto the highway. Then, maybe ten or fifteen minutes later, I'd pull into the parking lot of the liquor store in my own neighborhood and buy a quart of Jack Daniel's, with no memory, none at all, of the fearsome battle I had just fought with myself only moments before.

It goes without saying that Kathi and I were unhappy. She was unhappy with me, and I was unhappy with her unhappiness with me, so I raged at her. I was creating a distance between us, then accusing her of withdrawing. I was afraid: of intimacy, of responsibility, of the truth. I was afraid I would have to stop drinking.

One day, when Robert was about to turn four, we were at a dinner party given by a friend. After dinner the three adult couples were sitting in the living room around a glass coffee table filled with desserts when Robert came reeling into the room, knocking against the walls, with a plastic cup in his hand, pretending to be drunk. He staggered over to me, presented me the cup, and in his clear, high, three-year-old's voice said, "Here, Daddy! This is for you! It's whiskey!" I took the cup from him, threw back my head, and laughed. What a clever kid!

Everyone else, silent, was looking at the floor. Three months later, I walked into my first AA meeting.

&

Soon after we moved to Massachusetts, I met a guy I'll call Charlie, a psychologist, the father of two sons who seemed to adore him. As a young father myself, I saw him as a guide. Charlie knew where to rent boats to go out on the flats after flounder. He knew when the bluefish were running and what they were biting and the best spots to surfcast. "See that rocky point there? The blues drive the baitfish toward that shelf, and they have no choice but to turn toward shore, so the blues only need to swim in an inverted V to corral them. Then it's a bloodbath. They're pack hunters, like wolves."

I was more of a freshwater guy myself, not having seen the ocean until I was eighteen. One day we were heading to the North Shore to fish and, being a new father, I was having a hard time with my dad—with him, with my memory of him, and with my idea of him. I was determined to be what I thought of as a better father—not more loving, my father's affection was never in doubt, but more discerning about the influences my son would contend with, more critical of the masculine culture that I felt had crippled me in ways I was only beginning to understand. I thought that if my father would only be more forthcoming, talk about his boyhood, his time as a paratrooper in World War II, his marriage to my mother, I might get to know him as a man, not just Dad, or now, Poppop. I might come to appreciate his complexity and find a way to love him as complexly. Charlie seemed to enjoy being a father, and besides, he was a psychologist, so I thought I'd talk with him.

"Your father doesn't want you to know him."

"I don't understand."

"What's not to understand? He doesn't want you to get to know him."

"I mean know who he really is."

"He doesn't *want* you to know who he really is! Come on, that's obvious!"

"You think he's hiding something?"

"He's hiding who he is."

"Why?"

"Why not? Look, you are grown up, gone away, married, you have a kid. The guy doesn't owe you anything. He raised you. That's enough. Be grateful and leave the poor bastard alone."

"I'd just like to get to know him better."

"Tough shit."

That conversation shook me. I don't remember much else about that fishing trip. I spent the whole afternoon and evening trying to accept what Charlie had said. It wasn't until a dozen years later, however, that I understood. One day, Charlie's wife got a call from an irate husband. Turns out Charlie'd been a tomcat the whole marriage. It was, of course, shattering for his wife and worse, if that's possible, for his two sons, both young men now.

"The guy doesn't owe you anything. He raised you. That's enough."

Going through my father's things, I come upon a folder marked "army stuff" that contains a photo he sent home to his parents, and a number of flimsy and yellowing documents.

SAVE THIS FORM.
IT WILL NOT BE REPLACED IF LOST.

These words are from my father's "Separation Qualification Record," dated January 31, 1946, from which I learn that my father spent three months in basic training, two months training as a "Rifleman 745," four months as an "Automatic Rifleman 746," a month in paratrooper training ("Student Parachute 629"), and finally sixteen months as a "Rifleman 7745." Under "Summary of Military Occupations," it says:

TITLE—DESCRIPTION—
RELATED CIVILIAN OCCUPATION

RIFLEMAN 7745—Jumped from airplane by parachute. Loaded, aimed and fired a rifle to destroy enemy personnel and to assist in capturing and holding enemy positions. Placed fire upon designated targets or distributed fire upon positions as situation demanded. Trained in use of hand weapons including rifle, automatic rifle, rocked [*sic*] launcher, rifle grenade launcher, bayonet, trench knife and hand grenades. Advantage of camouflage, cover and concealment, intrenching, recognition and following arm and hand signals, recognition of enemy personnel, vehicles and aircraft. Familiar with hand to hand fighting techniques.

That's it, the text fills the box. No room, I suppose, for "Related Civilian Occupation." It makes me sad. And angry on my father's behalf: what could he have possibly taken, this young man, into civilian life from such a curriculum? When he was drafted, my father was an engineering student at the Virginia Military Institute. I suspect that he was there in the hope that he would be perceived, at least potentially, as an engineer, as too valuable to the war effort to become cannon fodder, trying to demonstrate he had some brains. After the war, my father never returned to school. I don't know why.

Once discharged, he never again flew in an airplane. Not even later in his life when air travel had become commonplace. When driving six or seven hours became too much for him, we encouraged him to fly. No way. I'd try to joke with him about it, cajoling him with the reassurance that no jumpmaster would require him to "Sta-a-a-nd up! A-a-a-n-n-d, HOOK up!" His lip curled and he tucked his chin for just a moment like a dog about to snap, just before he recovered with a grin, not quite a smile. "Yeah, I never did LAND in one of the damn things." And I knew, again, there was still a tender spot there, some unhealed lesion of his spirit. Seeing him flinch and nearly growl, I felt my own untreated injuries, still raw and alert to his mood. Both of us had learned—I learning mostly from him—the *advantage of camouflage, cover, and concealment.*

&

Because I am a father, and because both my son and my daughter are older than my father was when he was so grievously betrayed, along with a critical mass of his generation, by his century's savagery; and because my grandson's father, Jamaican-born, black, along with a critical mass of *his* generation, is in prison, I think about these things—and even about my father's life—more from a paternal than a filial vantage. And because I am a grandfather, I do my considering more from an ethical if no less personal angle. I hope to see my grandson become a young man; I hope to help raise him to adulthood. I'm sixty-one as I write this, not very old for a man of my generation, but there's no guarantee.

I look at this photo of my father and I see my son's face, not mine, although sometimes I glimpse my father in the mirror these days. My father is younger in this photograph than my son as I write this, but I see they have the same mouth, the same tight smile, a little crooked, as if always just about to make a wisecrack. They have the same round cheeks, the same tamed curls, the same jawline. In the photo, I see a boy, not a line on his smooth face. I wonder if he even needed a razor.

He's in a uniform, pressed wool, crisp lapels, brass buttons. A medal dangles from one flap pocket. This must have been on the occasion of his completing basic training, or jump school.

There is no fear in this young man's eyes. He knows, of course, that he is going to war. And there's nothing of the posed hardness you sometimes see in such photos. His face is open, proud as a kid on his first-communion day.

And it is only viewing the photo this time that I am able, for the first time, to detach myself enough from his gaze to notice that in the lower right-hand corner he has written:

To my parents,
Dick

I was Dick Jr. growing up. Or Dickie. I could say I always hated it, but that's not true. The teasing started in about fifth or sixth grade. Friends would call and my mother would ask, "Do you want big Dick or little Dick?" Once I remember playing cards on a rainy Saturday: war, or maybe crazy eights, with some friends on the living room rug. My mother was on the phone nearby, evidently talking to an old friend she hadn't seen in some years because we heard her— we all heard her—exclaim, "And you should see how big my Dick has grown!" Cards flew through the air! I wasn't exactly secure at that age, and I couldn't join the hilarity. My friends, having witnessed the hot shame and stifled anger of my response, did their best the rest of the afternoon, but they just couldn't help themselves. Now and again a snort would escape somebody and that would set everyone laughing again while I stewed. "Come on, just play the game! It's your turn."

In Stephen Ambrose's introduction to David Kenyon Webster's *Parachute Infantry*, he quotes Paul Fussell: "It can't happen to me. I am too clever/agile/well-trained/good-looking/beloved/tightly laced, etc.," to ever get hit. After a few hours or days or weeks of combat, that attitude gives way to: "It can happen to me, and I'd better be more careful. I can avoid the danger by watching more prudently the way I take cover/dig in/expose my position by firing my weapon/

keep extra alert at all times, etc.," then comes the realization that "It is going to happen to me, and only my not being there (on the front lines) is going to prevent it."

I don't believe my father's denial system was sufficiently developed for him to have experienced that "It can't happen to me" phase. His brother Francis was already a Nazi prisoner by then, his survival depending on his ability to prove he was not a Jew. It was late in the war, although it was uncertain how long it would go on, and my father had known any number of other young men who had lost their lives.

My father's personality was shaped by that war, by his sense of himself as a soldier. During his final illness, late into a hospital stay of several weeks, when he began to experience some nighttime dementia, as older people often do when hospitalized, his delusions turned on the theme of warfare, of having been captured. He'd tear out the IVs, leave his room, and creep down the brightly lit halls to the door, all three hundred pounds of him, in nothing but a hospital johnny. Discovered, he would fight the nurses, repeating, "I have to get back to my unit! I have to get back to my unit!"

So what does it mean that, according to my research, he was in a unit that never saw combat?

It was my father's good fortune in World War II not to be sent to the front. When two-thirds of his division, the 515th, was transferred to the 82nd and 101st divisions for the Normandy invasion, his orders were to remain with the 515th at Fort Benning, Georgia. There were not enough planes to transport all of them. The 515th would be part of a later assault to be launched against the Fuhrer's bunker. After a short time in England, they were sent to France, to Le Havre, where they received the order to parachute into Germany. However, ground forces moving up from the south were more successful than expected, the jump was deemed unnecessary, and the order was revoked. They returned to the United States to prepare for the invasion of Japan. That August, the explosion of the atomic bombs over Hiroshima and Nagasaki obviated the need for the 515th.

Luck: I'm haunted by the fact that I would not be here if it weren't for these circumstances. There's no making sense of it; in fact, it drives home the point that we are all accidents and the result of accidents, luck. My brothers Bob and Mike were afflicted with muscular dystrophy. I was not. Nor was my brother Joe. To argue that there is a reason, unseen but glimpsed, in the events of history, is self-serving foolishness. To argue that we can't see the reason because we are the reason is to turn reason on its head and insist that the world exists only as the instrument of our narcissism. Our metaphysics cannot rest on solipsism and self-congratulation. Humility, it seems to me, ought to be considered the highest virtue since only humility, knowing that one's good fortune is only that, good luck and nothing else, makes possible whatever clarity can be had. Luck, not superior strength, wisdom, agility, intelligence, or virtue. Luck. Assertions to the contrary are suspect to me. There may be untruths we need to tell ourselves, but they are nonetheless fictions. *Don't be fooled.*

I think that some part of me was disappointed to find that my father was never in combat. Outrageous to feel that way, I know, but war propaganda shaped the world I was born into, and the remnants of that orientation, like the boots, helmets, ammo cases, belts, and uncharged grenades at the Army/Navy store, the surplus, the accoutrements of war, shaped the aesthetics and ethics of the people who raised me.

The Army/Navy store was on Seventh Street near Sears,

Roebuck, where somebody had used tar to draw a strike zone on the blond brick wall so we could play fastball in the parking lot on Sundays and in the early summer evenings, except for Thursdays, when the store stayed open until nine.

All that gear, all that surplus, the rubber gas masks, the cargo belts, the canteens, the collapsible shovels, the hard-toed high shined boots, the woolen olive sweaters, the helmets and soft caps, even the badges and medallions, were not, it occurs to me now, used things left behind when peace was declared. They were provisions for a war that ended soon after the first atomic bombs were dropped on Japan, equipment for a war that would now be play-acted by pubescent infantries in the woods and fields behind the church and school.

I held my father in awe because he had been a paratrooper. He had a yearbook, something like a college yearbook, from jump school at Fort Benning. The inside covers front and back were the same glorious photo of a sky filled with pearly silk parachutes, so radiant in sunlight that it surprised me years later, as an adult, to find that the photos were black-and-white. His dog tags, shoulder patches, ribbons, and regalia were sacred things to me, although my father kept them in a tangled heap in his junk drawer. Among my father's tools, downstairs in the cellar, there was his bayonet: a long knife that slid from a hard sheath, an object of masculine wonder. A ring on the handle would have clasped it to the barrel of a Browning automatic rifle, called, simply, a BAR. "Fix bayonets!" was a command we were all familiar with from TV and movies, a command that meant, "This is it!" Or "Here we go!" There would be no mercy, the combat would be at close quarters, bloody, and to the death.

The bayonet was grooved and sleek. There were faded stains on it: rust or blood? What was it my father said when

I asked him? He always put me off when I asked about the war. For a while I convinced myself—in the absence of any information from him—that he kept it because it had saved his life: there were many scenarios for this fantasy, all of them borrowed from TV and film.

In one scene my father has just parachuted into a field at night and crawled past a French barn. His presence, flat against the side of the barn and then as a shadow among cows tethered close together for the night, sets off a commotion among the cows, goats, and chickens that brings a German sentry for a look. There is a way, I know from the films and from my Attack Force and Sergeant Rock comic books, to kill quietly, stealthily, so as not to alarm anyone. My father steps from the shadows, and with this very bayonet, he slits the man's throat so cleanly that he cannot cry out.

In another fantasy my father is in a foxhole and has time only to raise his BAR quickly to a priapic angle as a bestial German soldier throws himself upon what he thought was my father's sleeping form.

Oh, there were plenty of these. One even involved my father throwing the magic blade—*whoosh*—so that a Nazi grabs at his chest, a shocked look on his face, and falls, just as he was about to do some foul thing I didn't fully understand to a tiny French girl. This is, of course, impossible; bayonets were not made to be thrown, the balance would be off, the hilt much heavier than the blade.

Another fantasy scene from boyhood, again from the movies: my father is on his belly crawling across a minefield. I can see the beads of sweat on his frowning brow—courtesy no doubt of a close-up of Sergeant Rock's square-jawed, deeply shadowed face—and he's gently probing the ground in front of him, the blade of the bayonet inserted again and again at an acute angle. "Tick." The sound of metal on metal.

He reaches over his shoulder exactly the way an archer would reach for an arrow, and withdraws a small red flag on a wire he places in the ground to mark the mine's position. The rest of his unit is waiting and watching from the edge of the wood, anxiously, while he risks his life to find them safe passage from the trap the Germans have sprung on them. He crawls forward again, proceeding by inches, probing and flagging. When the Germans arrive at dusk to demand their surrender, trapped there in the wood, they will be gone.

No doubt somebody could chart these notions across the filmography of the fifties. Maybe I ought to do it, now that almost all of it's been put on DVDs. But that would be beside the point. The imagery, the action, the violent conflict of good and evil, were lodged inside me, along with the wish for a set of circumstances in which to prove myself heroic.

When we played war in the fields and woods behind the school, I was allowed to wear the bayonet's green scabbard, almost the length of a sword relative to my four feet of ferocious fantasy, but the bayonet was forbidden and, in fact, disappeared for many years, no doubt as a result of my unhealthy and dangerous interest in it. Later, as an adult visiting my father, I was rooting around for a pair of pliers in a drawer in an old wooden chest in the basement, and there it was, not much the worse for wear except for the broken tip, and the entire romance came back to me: the World War II movies with my father in the starring role. I asked him, again, why he still had it. Surely he'd confide to his fifty-year-old son what he could not or would not tell his ten-year-old child. "What? That damn thing? I don't know. Last time I used it was to cut ceiling tiles for the upstairs bathroom."

Most of my friends' fathers had been to war. One of our neighbors walked with a kind of hop, another with a cane.

A man across the street wore a sock on the stump of his arm and once joked with us that he'd wished they could have found his arm; he wanted to put it under his pillow for the arm fairy. "What do you think I'd get for that?" That was the bitterest laugh I'd ever heard. Some were like the guys in the movies who jumped on a grenade to save their friends, only they jumped on a bottle of beer, curled around it, and it slowly exploded over the next twenty five or thirty years while their kids, who saw them as irascible losers, were spared the worst of what they might have suffered had their fathers enacted with full force the violence they brought home with them instead of hiding out at the American Legion or the VFW. Sometimes the grenade was not a bottle of booze, just a sucking emptiness, a black hole, an insatiable maw. "You don't want to know," they kept saying. They meant, "I don't want you to know. I don't want you to have to know." Where is the memorial to those guys? What would it look like?

At the Army/Navy store my father explained to me what each shoulder patch, arranged in cubbyholes like a postman's sorting rack, stood for. They were all beautiful to me, tough as carpet and woven into brilliant colored designs: the ones I could already recognize, such as the 101st Airborne's screaming eagle, or the 82nd Army Airborne AA on a blue circled red field. And the many others my father knew: the maroon and black of the Blackhawk Division; the 66th Infantry's black panther on a gold field; the 63rd, the Blood & Fire Division, a bloody sword against a background of flames.

It was there in a dark and narrow aisle in the back of the store that my father explained to me the beautiful practicality of the paratroopers' jump boots. He held up a pair, black and smooth as polished onyx, the long tongue a deep royal blue on the inside, toes shined "so you could see your face in them" and reinforced eyelets all the way up, no buckles or even the slightest protrusion on them anywhere, nothing on which the strings of your chute could catch. He caressed the boots, smelled them, held one to my cheek, "feel how smooth."

They had none in my size, barely a man's size, only a pair of infantry boots, part leather, part canvas, with the double buckle around the ankle, and he bought me those although he seemed to disapprove of them somehow, the boots of the foot soldiers, not the sleek and smooth leather that made paratroopers stand out.

I knew from the division's yearbooks, which I pored over constantly, that trainees wore high-top Converse sneakers until they were given, with much ceremony, and after successful completion of their training, their very own jump boots, which each man kept polished and well oiled to keep the leather supple.

"You get a blister, it could slow you down. You could get killed because you didn't take care of your boots."

I took this all in. The world was a dangerous place but one could take precautions. Lucky for me—and I felt it, felt grateful—I had my father, who shared what he had learned with me. He would keep me safe if I followed his directions.

When we could not play war with our canteens and utility belts and helmet liners and Frannie's dead grenade that had been turned into a cigarette lighter; when we were not shooting at each other or crawling across the ground on our stomachs, sliding our wooden bayonets into the ground at acute angles, inching our way forward through imagined mine fields, covered in branches and leaves for camouflage; when it was raining, our mothers yelling, You're not going out there you'll catch your death of cold!—we played war indoors.

First of all there was the card game, the simplest card game we knew: flip over one card at a time and the higher-valued card wins. If two cards of the same value were turned over, you had a war: one card down and the other would decide the battle. When the battle was decided, you turned over the first card to see what you'd won—you never knew, it might be a high-value card that would help in the next war, maybe not. In any case, the game was over when total victory had been achieved: one person had all the cards.

Another indoor war involved our "army guys." Everybody had a bag of hard green rubber soldiers for these wars, and the bag included not only soldiers standing, sitting, or lying on their bellies shooting, but also tanks, trucks, artillery, and tiny machine guns. Indoors we perfected the sounds of the weapons: rifle fire, machine guns, explosions, as we knocked over the enemy's soldiers who, once deployed, could not retreat.

Everything about that postwar boyhood was colored by the war that had just ended. What our fathers would not tell us we imagined, and Hollywood was there to help. As soon as the sun came out we headed for the battlefield with its foxholes to dig, its trees to climb and snipe from, its boulders to take cover behind.

What we could not tell one another but what I believe we all felt was that we were playing with death, playing at dying. After all, we were told, daily, that another war was imminent, and that this time there was little chance of survival. The communists had their missiles trained on us and those mushroom clouds in the photos of Japan would soon be pillaring upward on our own horizon as they had already done again and again in our nightmares. Besides, killing was merely hitting a target, like an icy snowball clanging a street sign or the satisfying *thwack* of a spongeball in the strike zone. Killing wasn't the mystery; dying was the greater challenge to the imagination. You'd cry out, stagger, fall as dramatically as you could muster. Then you could lie in the grass and be more silent than you would ever otherwise have any excuse to be, high grasses arching over you, leafhoppers of neon green crisscrossing your vision, a sky of ozone blue above you as you lay there trying to ignore the itch of a bug on your neck, feeling the boredom setting in, hearing the shouts and calls and play-acting of your friends nearby.

We didn't care that everything was way too big. "Neat!" we said. We didn't care a bit if we flapped when we ran, our canteens and shovels and cartridge belts falling down from our hipless waists, the chin-strapped helmet liners wobbling on our heads, because these were not toys; these things were real!

We would grow into them. Our war was still in the future, the war that would turn some of us into cynics, that would rip apart families, that would send some abroad in search of safety, and that would chisel more than fifty thousand boyhood dreamers out of their lives and onto black basalt wedged like a blade in the heart of our native land.

I remember a Memorial Day weekend many years later. We were riding in the car, Kathi and me and the kids, possibly going on a visit to my father in Pennsylvania. Perhaps we had been listening to news on the radio because suddenly our son Robert, five years old, riding in the backseat with his baby sister, made a declaration: "War is bad!" His mother and I agreed, both of the generation that came of age in 1968. "But Poppop fought in a war," Robert offered, "he fought in a parachuter war."

It was a kind of query so we answered him by explaining, carefully, that sometimes a person has to decide between two things that both seem wrong and that some people fought in the war because they wanted to stop the killing that was already going on. He was quiet for a long time. He fell asleep. When he woke he rubbed his eyes, stretched, yawned, and said, "Tell me again."

"Tell you what again?"

"Tell me about the time when Poppop came down out of the sky and stopped the war."

Just a few years later, when Robert was in second grade, Operation Desert Wind became Operation Desert Storm and the brothers, fathers, and uncles of several kids in his school were called to active duty and sent to the Persian Gulf. The principal decided that the kids deserved some reassurance, and someone to answer their questions about what was going on, so she assembled a schoolwide program that featured the local recruitment officer from the Army Reserve.

But I was more concerned with a nine-year-old boy watching a man in a crisp uniform with colorful medals above his heart, standing straighter than he'd ever seen anyone stand before, with his hat under his arm, his brass buttons shining, wearing white gloves. Were I that boy I would be trying to narrow my eyes, jut out my jaw, stand up straight, and quickly become somebody else: the man up there on stage saying we live in the greatest nation on earth and that liberty must always have heroes to defend it from its enemies. And all those bloody et ceteras.

&

The visiting room is a large, stark room of beige ceramic brick, with blue seats in rows fixed to the floor. One of the guards points me to a seat, and after about ten minutes, Damion comes through the door and checks in at the desk where a guard sits on a raised platform. I see him scanning the crowded room so I raise my hand; he beams for a moment before returning to his blank prison visage, a mask to wear as he makes his way past other prisoners and their visitors, other prisoners he may need to be wary of, whom he must communicate with here—by looking or not looking at them, by nodding or not, by his carriage, his walk on his way to where I sit. Social tripwires I can't see are everywhere around him. Asked about this, he will shrug. "It is what it is."

Prison is a box in which we put our nightmares, our worst fears; prisoners are the actors we've chosen to cast in the roles of malefactors. (And how do we audition them?) The whole place is the architectural expression of self-righteousness. Each of the guards is free, within wide parameters, to exercise his personal biases, doubtless believing he is operating as a force for order, safety, virtue, law. One of the guards seems to have appointed himself Damion's nemesis, undermining him at every opportunity. According to Veronica, it is because she and Damion are an interracial couple. "We will be sitting across from each other, holding hands, and that jerk will come walking down the row past couples making out and—almost fucking!—and warn us that any more intimate contact will end the visit." This same guard has repeatedly written up Damion for offenses so minor (and in at least one case fictional) they are preposterous. But when it comes to jobs inside the prison—in the kitchen, laundry, etc.—jobs for which one gets "good time," i.e., time off one's sentence, it is the number of infractions, not their severity or even veracity, that will disqualify you.

I get it that it's a shitty job. I get that their authority is being tested every day. I get that in some important ways they are as dehumanized by the situation as the inmates. Still, one can feel their contempt for anyone who is there who doesn't need to be. Visitors, yes. But especially volunteers, the army of naïve do-gooders who seem always to be convinced of a contagious virtue they are carrying. They only make things worse with their bullshit.

I was one of them years ago. In this very prison, among others. I volunteered with the Alternatives to Violence Program, or AVP, but only on two weekends. Both times I was the only male on the team of five. Mostly I stood off to the side and watched the women present the material. The program is designed so that after several weekends you become certified to teach the curriculum; after a few more, you're certified to lead a team.

I recall returning from the first weekend disturbed and uncomfortable, but it was hard for me to grasp what was bothering me, especially since it was my first time inside a prison, but I sensed it had something to do with the approach my AVP colleagues were taking. Still, who was I to criticize?

So I returned a couple of weekends later for the second session of the course. At one point, when the lead teacher turned to write on a newsprint pad mounted on an easel—"de-escalate"—one of the inmates caught my eye and nodded in her direction, making a lewd gesture with his hand and mouth. None of the women saw it. He looked at me, all but winked at me: we know the score, don't we? I did nothing. Which put me on his side, I suppose.

And yet, that moment, and that inmate's vulgar schoolboy gesture, snapped me out of any illusion that we were getting through to any of the men in the room. The immaturity and misogyny of that moment, not to mention the look I received from the inmate and the complicity of my inaction, combined in a way I recognized. For all of our differences, we men in that room by and large had shared the standard-issue American boyhood. In that curriculum, violence, not so much hidden as disguised—as athleticism, as patriotism, as ambition—is of the essence. And so I came to believe that the women were starting from the wrong set of assumptions. These prisoners were not men who had strayed from the path, not at all; they had learned their culture's lessons, our culture's lessons, all too well; they were the guys who got an A in the course, and had they had other opportunities, other arenas in which to deploy their gladiatorial training, they might have been CEOs or senators. They would get an A in this course, too, because after all, telling women what you have figured out they want to hear is also part of the hidden curriculum of boyhood.

I seldom hear anything that sounds like the truth about boyhood. I myself have been lying about boyhood ever since it ended. Not that I can point to a moment when it ended. I used to do that, too, tell about the moment I became a man, but that was another lie. As I work to strip away the lies, I see why it was I needed each of them. Or maybe as I outgrow the need for each lie, it becomes clear to me for what it is, becomes defined and articulate, and slips away, but not before I get a glimpse of all the other lies—and a few truths, too—it was connected to. Sometimes it feels as if I am unraveling, but I no longer think that's a bad thing. Maybe when I'm done unraveling there will be time enough remaining to make something new of myself, something more of my own design. If not, then at least I will have spent my time on a project of my own, quixotic though it may have been.

Remaking oneself. Isn't that what prison affords the opportunity to do? Wasn't that its original purpose? Is this not called a "correctional institution"? In reality, I doubt that society wants more Gramscis, Dostoyevskys, Malcolms.

About a year after my AVP experience, I was given the

chance to lead a men's group at "The Farm," Concord's pre-release facility. It was not an AA meeting or really anything like it. But it was called Tools of Recovery and based on a curriculum a local pastor and clinician had devised. The term "recovery" was understood broadly. When I first agreed to lead this group, the program was designed as an eight-week course. It usually took five or six weeks for the men to finish giving voice to their resentment at being incarcerated. During that time my role was to listen. I recall one man doing time for possession of a handgun:

"In my neighborhood? Where I live? Know what we call a nigger with no gun?

"Dead."

The second time I ran the course, I lengthened it to ten weeks. Finally, it found its real length—twelve weeks. I remember one guy in an early class who really helped me to shape subsequent discussions. Many of the men had children, and we were talking about what it takes to be a good father. Some were angry that their children's mothers never brought them for a visit. Others were remorseful about missing years of their kids' growing up. But this guy was thinking of his own father. "My father?" he said, "my father? I fuckin' hate that guy! I fuckin' hate him! But I fuckin' love him, too. Y'know what I mean?" Or maybe it was the other way around. I honestly don't remember. What I recall is the ferocity of his emotion and how utterly deflated he was a moment later. The oscillation between a hateful bitterness and an angry love is exhausting.

As Damion comes close and smiles, I see my grandson in his face. I rise and hug him, both of us mumbling, "How are you? Good to see you. Good to see you, too. I'm good. I'm good." I believe I can see the boy he was, a child still so present it's heartbreaking, the boy who deserved so much more than he was given, and I can watch his face, first puzzled and then closing, as he comes to know, in some wordless, unacknowledged way, that I have been looking *into* him, that I am trying to bring what he's told me of his life here, now, to this encounter, that I want to know him. I have embarrassed him, I think, even frightened him a little.

Over the course of several visits, we have talked about prison life, legal matters, Jamaica, Veronica, Robert, Kathi, our conversation punctuated by stories about D, who is now four and offering hypotheses for everything he doesn't understand. I bring him the latest funny thing he said, or something I have observed, or else Damion recounts D's last visit to him there at the prison. We have talked about our fathers, about being beaten by our fathers, about our disappointment in them and our attachment to them, about our confusion, about our love and fury.

The man next to us, two chairs away, is seated across from a woman I take to be his mother. She is feeding him, that is, she's bought him a sandwich from the vending machine and microwaved it. Steam escapes as he opens the plastic bag. The smell is not appetizing, but he takes a big bite, thanks her with his mouth full, chewing.

I tell Damion what D said to me a few days before. The two of us lay on the living room rug while I taught him the coins: pennies, nickels, dimes, quarters. Sometimes he called nickels "nipples" and dimes "diamonds." I tell him how just that morning he drew a picture of a playground. And that I said that when someone is going to build a playground, they always draw a picture first.

"Like a map!" D said, and I saw his pride and pleasure at another concept clicking into place. I thought I might offer the word blueprint, but thought better of it. Map was just fine. Damion is smiling, slowly shaking his head from side to side. "That kid's a trip," he says. "The other night I called Veronica and he answered the phone."

"Yeah, he's doing that now. He races to the phone to be the one to answer it."

"But get this. He says to me, 'Daddy, can you come over tonight?'"

"'D!' I said, 'you know I can't come over there. I have to stay here.'"

"'Daddy?' he says."

"I said, 'What?'"

"He says, 'Why are you in jail?'"

"I'm thinking, What the . . .'"

Damion admits he wasn't ready for this question. Until very recently, D was content to tell everyone his daddy lived in a castle, a big castle. Now, telling this, Damion's blinking back tears.

"I told him we could talk about that when I get out of here. 'I'll tell you when I come home,' I said. 'I promise.'"

"'Why won't you tell me now?' he says to me. I'm not sure what to say. I mean, can you believe this kid? At four years old? So I say, 'I will. I will tell you. When it's time. Let me talk to your mommy now.' Then the line was silent. I can hear somebody breathing, so I'm like, 'Veronica?'"

"'No. It's still me, Daddy. Tell me why you are in jail. Tell me now.'" Telling me this, he smiles and shakes his head with pride in this exasperating little boy, but he's sniffing and swallowing hard.

"'Because I had a gun,' I said to him."

"'Did you shoot somebody?' he asks me. He wants to know if I'm a bad guy."

"I'm like, 'No, no. I never shot nobody. I would never want to shoot nobody. Never.'"

"Then he says, 'But guns are bad?'"

"'Yes, guns are bad!' I tell him. 'That's why I'm in jail.'"

"'Daddy?' he says."

"I mean, the kid won't let up. So I say, 'What? Are you going to let me speak to your mother?'"

"He's like, 'Daddy?'"

"And I'm all messed up by this whole conversation and I say, 'What?'"

"'Thank you for telling me why you're in jail,' he says. 'I love you.' Can you believe it?"

"So I say, 'I love you too, D. Now let me talk to Mommy.' Man!" Damion's leaning forward now, elbows on his knees; he sniffs and collects himself, looks up and smiles. "That kid's a trip."

And I don't swap him the next story, the one I brought with me that I thought he'd like, the way I used to bring my brother Bobby stories of things I'd seen living in New York. I feel like an idiot for not seeing how cruel it would have been. Kathi and I had taken D to the Peabody Essex Museum in Salem to see some Native American dancing as part of an exhibit. D was rightly impressed by the hoop dance. "How does he do the magic with the hoops?" And it was, certainly, magical: hoops, in several combinations, became wings of birds, butterflies, a ball, a cage, a horse. I didn't get to see D's face since he was on my shoulders; Kathi says he was enthralled. He also enjoyed an exhibit about water. On the way home we talked about the hoop dance. Kathi said the dancer mentioned during the Q&A that his father had taught him the dance.

"When I was a little, little boy," D said from the back seat, "my father taught me things. I have a father, too."

"Yes. Yes you do!" said Kathi.

"And when I was a little boy, a little, little boy, he taught me lots and lots of things."

Silence.

Instead I tell Damion how just that morning we went to the playground in our neighborhood, where there are always tricycles and wagons left by neighbors whose kids have outgrown them. I tell him about D wrapping his arms and ankles around the thin and supple branch of a young maple gone to orange, and hanging there just a few feet from the ground. "Look at me, Grandpa!"

But I don't know how to convey my experience of the morning. A wind came up and blew leaves from the treetops. "Look at me, Grandpa!" And I looked at him knowing, deeply, that we are all here for only some brief season of seasons we have no name for. "Life" is too commonplace, and carries no feeling. "Lifespan" has a span in it, a bridge, a concept I can't always muster the faith for. Call it our portion, a single share of the plenitude of time, with little or nothing to do with anything but love, partaking of everything that ever was or will be.

Damion and I just grin at each other until he says, again, "That kid's a trip."

&

All my life I've carried a sense that the world is beyond our knowing, beyond our capacity to understand. Since the age of eight or nine I have awakened every morning to the questions, "Why Bobby and not me? Why Bob and Mike, but not me, or Joe?" What cosmic lottery decides that? What God decrees it? I cannot refuse this roaring chord of fear, awe, gratitude, and sadness, it has been the roar in my ears ever since. It is, I believe, the elemental form of the religious impulse.

It seems to me now that my ninth year was a turning point. My brother Bobby, eight, was no longer able to walk.

I remember little about this colossal change in our lives. My parents told me nothing. I remember being punished for my impatience with Bobby, "Come on!" I'd say, and he would whine, "I can't. I can't!" I couldn't parse the fury I felt then, couldn't tell the difference between rage at what was happening to him and anger at my brother himself. He was moved out of our bedroom, into the fold-out sofa downstairs and—When did it arrive? How is it suddenly one day there, as if it belonged in the spot—next to the sofa, foot rest up, its scissored chassis folded closed, the wheelchair, chrome and green vinyl. What could my parents have said? How could they have explained what must have only then been sinking in?

Yes, everything changed that year. Of course I was not a self-conscious observer, so to say that everything changed is a judgment I make now, sifting through memories. And the lack of memories, the paucity of physical impressions, is surprising to me. I have such vivid sensual recall of so much of my childhood that I must take this poverty as a sign of just how confused and abstracted I had become. What was happening to my brother had a name but no meaning, a terrible reality but no explanation.

Could my parents have taken me aside, a nine-year-old, and said, "We know you and your brother have been playmates all your lives, but that's over"? Could they have explained that Bobby was never going to walk again? That he would grow weaker and weaker now until he died? As I said, I have few specific memories of this change, so maybe they did try to tell me what was happening. Or maybe they did explain it to me but I didn't understand, or couldn't, or wouldn't. Or maybe they were trying to spare me the worst of it.

Or maybe—here I am ashamed at the narcissism of my

inquiry—maybe I was not their first concern, not the first of
their sons who needed an explanation.

&

Kathi's oncologist called to report that the second surgery
had gone well. Radiation would suffice; there was no need
for further surgery or chemo. She scheduled her treatments
for early in the morning five days a week, and continued to
teach her classes. As the weeks went on, fatigue became a
fact of life, along with radiation burns, patches of tender
purple skin, blisters. Salves, ointments, naps, and her ferocious commitment to her students kept her going.

I didn't know this at the time, but after that second surgery, Kathi had asked a friend if she could stay with her
for a while if she felt the need. Our house was too chaotic
and stressful. D, a year old, loved his grandmother intensely
and always wanted her to pick him up; Veronica was working hard as a floor nurse in a rehab hospital; I was working
two jobs and revising the book of stories I'd been writing;
the kitchen sink was always piled with pots and pans and
dishes, toys and books were strewn everywhere—there was
nowhere restful or even very private where Kathi could heal.

&

My father, the youngest of five children, was born August
29, 1925. That year saw the invention of the first mechani-
cal "televisor," precursor of the modern television. Calvin
Coolidge was president. The month before, in Tennessee,
John Scopes was convicted of teaching evolution in a public school. Al Jolson starred on Broadway, in blackface, in
Big Boy. Alcoholic beverages were illegal. Recently enacted
Child Labor Laws were being protested by anti-union
"right-to-work" legislators. It is staggering to think of the

technological changes my father witnessed during his life-time, and sobering to think we are still contending over science education, still largely divided by racism, still looking for ways to exploit, rather than reward, labor.

Our first television was second hand, a long, low piece of walnut furniture with a kind of window in front to protect the rounded and bulging screen, the olive drab of army fatigues. A flat wire called the lead-in wire connected the array of tubes inside the set to an antenna on the roof. On more than a few occasions when we had a snowy picture or a double image, my father would open the window nearest the TV, from which the lead-in wire ascended to the roof, and instruct me to tell him when the picture was in focus. He would climb the ladder to the roof, then turn the antenna while I yelled up from below, "That's better. That's better. Good! No! Too far! Too far!"

I remember one occasion when I'd yelled that the picture was good, but by the time my father came back down and stood in front of it, it wasn't. "I thought you said we had it."

"We did! We did! I don't know what happened."

"Oh, for Christ's sake," my father muttered. He smacked the side of the television hard, twice. "Try tugging on that lead-in wire." I leaned out the window and gave the wire a good yank. My father had been looking back and forth from the set to me; then he looked past me. "Shit!" he said, and I turned just in time to see the whole antenna, spidery and silver, land in the yard with a crash like an alien spaceship.

Keeping the television working was important, especially when Bobby became confined to his wheelchair. Whenever one of the sets, always second hand, "went on the fritz," my father would say, "I hope it's not the picture tube!" I understood the picture tube as the heart of the television; if it gave out, we'd have to find another one. The back of the TV was a piece of Masonite easily removed to reveal the array of tubes inside, and whenever there was trouble, my father would carefully remove them all, lay them out on the rug, and draw himself a diagram so he would know where each was to be returned. All of them were cylinders, of various heights and hefts, and each had a series of pins on the bottom where they were inserted into holes in the circuit board. Some were miniature inverted jars; others were round and smooth at the top like the glass case on an expensive cigar (not so very expensive, sold at the very same drugstore), and still others came to a little nipple on top. Inside were wires and bits of thin metal arranged in some magical way, perhaps kept separate by a disk of thin plastic, brown or green, that directed or redirected or modified the "juice" in a particular way that scientists had invented and other scientists, like my Uncle Bert, taking a night course to become a TV repairman, could understand.

But for the rest of us there was this trial and error, this wonderful errand I looked forward to, of bringing every last tube from the back of the set clinking gently in a rolled-up paper bag to the drugstore, where the tester stood just outside the wooden phone booth with its folding glass door and fat directory, half white, half yellow, hanging from a chain. The tester was an upright console with a large map or diagram above it with silhouettes, actual size, of each kind of tube. Next to each tube were numbers and letters corresponding to those on the tubes themselves (if you could find them) and a diagram of the arrangement of pins on its bottom. The console itself had an array of sockets for the tubes, also lettered and numbered.

The most important and interesting feature of the console, however, was the meter with its long and sensitive needle that would gauge—what? How "juicy" each tube still was? When you'd matched the tube to the diagram, found its number, checked the number on the tube, and plugged it into the correct socket on the console, the needle would slowly and surely sweep from its resting place in the red, left side of the spectrum, to the green, right side. Except when it didn't. That was a "dead soldier" my father said, the analogy twice removed from its literal source, arriving via the term for an empty bottle of beer. Then I knew that the reason the set had gone on the fritz right in the middle of *Your Show of Shows*, or *I Love Lucy*, or Ted Mack's *Original Amateur Hour*, was that the little soldier had given up the ghost. (I couldn't help but think of this ending as a kind of flash or pop like a sizzled flashbulb, which, come to think of it, was a tinier version of these tubes.)

Aha! I'd say, the needle in the red, entirely unpersuaded to budge, that's the one! Then I'd take it to the druggist, who would pull out a long drawer under the counter and rummage around until he found the box with the right number on it; always he'd slide the tube from the box and compare it to the dead one, just to be doubly sure it was the right one, and then I paid and, a job well done, headed back home to my father behind the television.

Sometimes he'd need help to put the tubes back in. "Argh, my goddamn fingers are too big. I don't want to take all those others out again. You try. Here. Can you see where it goes?" My father would shine the flashlight for me. "Can you get it?"

That this was the dawn of the electronic age, of the visual mediadrome and a new consensus reality, was lost on me, of course, but the seed of that knowledge was there in my wonder, holding one of the elegant glass-and-metal tubes up to the light: a machine without any moving parts. Magic.

&

The understandings of my father's generation, about war and women and violence and masculinity, codified and dramatized in film and television, and massively reinforced by advertising, became the culture in which I was raised, one that largely supplanted earlier values. To my father's generation, the destruction of Europe seemed to validate American ways.

Watching *Attack!* again, as an adult, I see that I didn't recall much about the story itself. Perhaps I hadn't yet acquired the skill or developed the cognitive apparatus to follow the narrative, only to absorb the imagery, that indelible imagery. I also had no way to know if the film was accurate in depicting a world without women and a war without civilians. It may be the distinguishing feature of my generation that we were the first in history to have the world portrayed for us, to us, at us, in such literal and convincing terms before we had any real experience of it.

I am not in the habit of clipping photos from newspapers, but I have kept a photograph that appeared in the *Boston Sunday Globe* at the start of the Afghan war, at this writing officially the longest in American history: a man, a Taliban fighter, is on the ground with no pants on, blood all over his legs, begging for his life. The photo captures, no doubt, the moment before his murder by victorious Northern Alliance soldiers who surround him, pointing their guns at the pathetic figure. From behind the main shooter in the center of the photo a man comes running with his palm held out in the universal sign for "Stop!" His face is horrified and his mouth is wide open so that if we could hear him we would understand, even without speaking a word of his language, that he is trying to give an order to desist, and that he already realizes he is too late. What is unclear, however, is whether his order is directed at the man with the gun or the man with the camera.

In 1938, in *Homage to Catalonia*, George Orwell wrote about his inability to shoot at a fascist courier because the man was "holding up his trousers with both hands as he ran . . . a man who is holding up his trousers isn't a 'Fascist,' he is visibly a fellow creature, similar to yourself, and you don't feel like shooting him." But here is a man without pants at all, his bloody robe hiked up around his waist, his hairy legs, his fat behind, his creatureliness undeniable. The blood on his legs, the gore on his hiked-up robe, may be evidence (it seems likely, given the horror on his face) that a mutilation has already taken place. Has he had his genitals shot off? The savagery of such an act would be consistent with the reported behavior of these men in other circumstances, for example, God help us, when entering villages, where wholesale rape, murder, and unimaginable acts of brutality are the order of the day.

Could it be that these warriors believe that what they are doing to the bare-assed bloody man in the photo is depriving him of his "manhood," which to them is more important than life itself? This delusion, of manhood—identified with the genitals as befits a phallic cult—as a state of being more important even than one's humanity, even than one's life, justifies any cruelty toward another male. When the phallus is turned into a weapon of power against female human beings, then the domination and indignity it represents is the whole point. Death, whose inverted view of everything has found expression in these actions, is, of course, the final, literal outcome.

The moral blindness of these men—along with the

blindness of those who flew jetliners into the World Trade Center or of those who fire missiles into wedding feasts— to the creatureliness of mothers and sisters and daughters and men who struggle to hold up their pants, is the triumph of a death-dealing metaphysics, the ascendance of symbol over reality. It seems fair then to ask what has changed since 1938, when Orwell could not pull that trigger. What has happened to men? In the years since then, mass mechanized death entered history and therefore our consciousness, and its terror has been passed down through the last several generations. The threat of instantaneous mass death, the theme of my cold war boyhood, does not inspire fellow feeling. This abiding fear, it hardly needs to be said, is a new thing in human history. And the horror experienced and survived by so many of our parents and grandparents has been bequeathed us in ways both visible and hidden, as violence and silence.

It is by now firmly understood that trauma repressed, denied its expression in language or art, will be passed on down the generations. In their landmark work, *History Beyond Trauma*, Francoise Davoine and Jean-Max Guadilliere contend that we inherit the trauma even of wars and other cataclysms distant in place and time. Unarticulated trauma is expressed in myriad behaviors that communicate trauma's injurious imprint from parent to child and shape the child's emotional expectations and psychic assumptions.

I was born three years and 364 days after the unconditional surrender of Nazi Germany, and three years and nine months after the first atomic bombs were dropped on the cities of Hiroshima and Nagasaki; three years, eight months, and four days after Japan surrendered to General MacArthur on the battleship USS *Missouri* on September 2, 1945. I remember seeing a picture of this when I was a boy, maybe in an old *Life* magazine still lying around the house, or a *National Geographic:* a couple of tables set up; General MacArthur there with the representatives of the Japanese emperor Hirohito; sailors, all leaning over rails, sitting on every deck of the ship looking as relaxed, animated, and happy as a theater packed full of kids for a typical feature at the Rialto, where on Saturdays we could get in for a can of beans or noodle soup to be donated to the Salvation Army food pantry. *It's over! It's over! Thank God, it's over!*

But relief at being alive is not the same as pleasure in being alive. A whole generation got to work restoring normalcy. But it had been a worldwide cataclysm; tens of millions of people had died; and a new and brutal idea emerged from that fact. Put simply, this toxic idea seems to be that the whole of the world is an arena in which one strives, that all the others one encounters there are adversaries or allies, and that there are necessarily winners, who live, and losers, who die.

It was Halloween, not long after September 11, 2001, and all over our neighborhood, along with jack o' lanterns and plastic skulls and cardboard witches, people were flying the colors. It was a windy day and everywhere flags were flapping like crazy, as if to tear themselves from poles and fly away, I thought, as if they understood they would be called upon, soon, to do their ugly duty again.

Our neighborhood makes a big deal of Halloween; small single-family houses built for returning Civil War vets are close together and make trick-or-treating easy. Angels, pirates, knights, superheroes, and, of course, witches and goblins go door to door for a couple of hours after dark, and people keep lots of candy on hand to drop in the bags and pillowcases the kids hold out. It struck me that year that the theme among the older boys, eleven or twelve, was decidedly military, lots of camouflage, camo paint on their faces, plastic rifles. One had a chain around another's neck as he dragged him up our front stairs: "He's my prisoner!" he said, and gave a yank on the chain. The other kid smiled and gave me a quick little wave. He had a turban on.

As always, as much as they could get away with given the fact that there were so many adults around, the older kids ran after the younger ones, trying to scare them. One young boy, in a skeleton suit from the store, ran past the front steps. "It's the tally bomb!" he cried out, looking to me for help. "The tally bomb is coming!"

I know it cannot be true, and I know that it is simplistic, but when I look at that photograph from the beginning of the Afghan war, I think that any and all alternatives to this, to what is being enacted in this photo, are good by contrast. Why argue about which ones are best? Would the man on the ground do that?

Ah, but if he weren't on the ground, he would be arguing for his position, as he no doubt had lately been doing, with a gun. Does he still believe, now, that there is another life? Now that he wants desperately to take a few more breaths? All I can do, all any of us can do now, is represented in the photo by that desperate running man with his palm held up: *stop!* But to whom is he, to whom am I, to whom are we, speaking? And why? I have no answer, do you? I am only a survivor, one among the many mourners.

&

I could write a guidebook to Allentown, but it would be filled with monsters. Its pleasures and joys would be secret and taken on the run by children running a gauntlet of post-traumatic adults swinging their fists, their religion, their dicks at them as they stumbled for daylight. Its pleasures and joys would be private and largely solitary: the ice-cold water of the Jordan Creek's rapids; the cool shade under the bell of a weeping willow, a stack of library books next to the couch, even the quiet of the church of an afternoon where I could retreat to incant the rosary and enchant myself with candles in red glass cups in rows and the sweet residue of incense in the air and the understanding faces of the sculptured saints that seemed to say they understood and who held their hands in ways that signaled, "Hush. You don't have to figure out how to say it, kid, I know. I know." What a relief.

Pleasure. Relief. Not being able to tell the difference is the precondition for addiction. The first time I tried to smoke a cigarette, I almost ripped my throat out coughing! I felt lightheaded and a little sick. I persisted, though. I could learn how to do it the way it was done in the movies and on TV. The way the adults did it. Cool. The way my father did it with me sitting on his lap while he blew smoke rings right through one another! Soon I could inhale without coughing and soon after that a craving began. The relief of that craving I called pleasure.

Why does my father remain such a mystery to me? I don't believe he had a terrible secret he kept from us, or that there is something he took to his grave that is yet to be discovered; it's more that he couldn't find a way to articulate his own complexity, his inner life, his essence. If he sometimes behaved as if he was ashamed, that doesn't mean he should have been. In any case, I think his inability to express the nature and variety of his feelings made me want to at least try to articulate mine.

When he worked at the Boys Club, my father would regularly bring home rubber molds for plaster of Paris "knickknacks"—first you turned the mold inside out and greased it thoroughly with Vaseline, then you popped it back right side out and poured it full of the mixture of powder and water you'd stirred to a pudding in a mixing bowl. The next day you could easily peel the rubber from the hardened figures and wipe them off with a damp rag. Then they were ready for painting, my favorite part. We certainly had some garish birds and rabbits and squirrels on the shelves and counters of our house!

One day, when I was in second or third grade, I think, he brought home a projector and a small reel of film. The Boys Club hambone team had been to a tournament and won second place. My father, as a counselor, was their coach. He had driven the Boys Club pickup truck with the kids in the back the hour to Philadelphia, and he was outraged that the judges had awarded first place to a team from Philly. As he threaded the projector he went on about how he thought his team had been robbed because he was white. "Couldn't give it to the kids with the white coach. How would that look? Hoo boy, those judges wouldn't have made it out of there alive! And I told them, too. I told the kids that as far as I was concerned, they won. Don't be fooled, I told them. You would have won if you had had a colored coach."

On the wall a dull rectangle of light with little shapes—dots, lines, streaks—and one permanent line from a crack in the plaster, then there they were, four young black boys in a row, seated on folding chairs. My father stood behind them. He leaned over and said something in one boy's ear. And (I remember this vividly) whatever he said caused the boy to break into a dazzling smile and shake his head from side to side as my father stepped out of the frame.

One boy began, drumming out a basic rhythm with his hands on his thighs. He called out:

Hambone, hambone have you heard?

Another boy joined in, slapping his thighs and chest in syncopation, the beat getting complicated, and responded:

Mama's gonna buy me a mockin' bird.

A third boy added his patting and clapping:

If that mockin' bird don't sing

And the fourth, the boy to whom my father had spoken, exploded in a virtuosic cascade of patting, slapping, clapping, and smacking while he sang back:

Mama's gonna buy me a diamond ring.

The four of them continued through the rest of the lyrics while the beat bounced, intricately braided, and the volume rose and fell, pulsing in a patterned flow.

If that diamond ring don't shine
Mama's gonna buy me a fishing line.
If that fishing line should break
Mama's gonna throw it in the lake.
If that water splash on me
Mama's gonna beat my b.u.t.

My father could not have known, nor would he have had the means to find out, hambone's origin as a response to cruelty, fear, hatred, and deprivation. His admiration for the skill of his team members was genuine, and he didn't understand why anyone might think otherwise. "People say you're not supposed to say they got rhythm. But why? They do! They do!" Had he known that the performance he so admired was a defiance of cultural erasure, he would have been all the more admiring. The drum, any drum, was forbidden. The healing drum was broken; the wedding drum, torn; the full-moon drum, in tatters; the mother drum, the father drum, splintered; no drums across the gorges, the hilltops, the waters; no signals, no meetings, no stories, no plans of escape or rebellion. And so the body became a drum, the body with its variety of pitches, its many textures, its hollows and surfaces and declivities, its expressive slaps and claps and pops and thumps and brushes; more sounds, almost, than a mouth, and just as much to say to those with ears to hear.

&

On the same visit to the Vermont Studio Center where I met my friend Letta, I shared a photo of my grandson with a Nigerian painter, Susana. We were in the dining hall, where I thought the food was delicious but where she could seldom eat anything without it upsetting her stomach. "This is your grandson?" Her puzzlement might have been that this gray old white man could be this child's grandfather. Or perhaps she meant—what? Nigerian English is inflected very differently from American, so it was hard for me to be sure what was behind the question. "In Nigeria, we say that your grandchildren are your ancestors."

"I thought it was the other way round." I laughed.

She continued to stare at the photo on my phone. She put her hand on my wrist, squeezed so I felt her urgency, pursed her lips and nodded, once.

"No. He is returned. He is your ancestor."

Once again I am challenged, in collision with a more capacious way of understanding the world that does not discount what language cannot convey, a view that describes time and eternity differently. It felt like stepping away from the wall, out onto the dance floor of the imagination. I have been taught to pretend that the imagination is not real, that it is not my constant companion, not an acceptable way to grasp reality, that it is a way of knowing that is to be left behind. The imagination is off limits to adults. An adult is someone who uses machines, who can drive. And an adult running a machine had better be where that machine is, whether it's a plane, or a lathe, or a saw.

Perhaps my grandfather was thinking of me when, a young man, he lost his forefinger to a circular saw? I still see his stump of an index finger though it is long since dust.

So, I am the ancestor of that hard little breaker boy on a wooden bench in the colliery shattering anthracite into smaller chunks? All right then: from here in the imagination, where these encounters can take place, I bless him. And here in the imagination he wipes a black streak across his face and feels, oddly, strengthened. Maybe he is thinking of a beautiful silk necktie that he saw on someone at church the previous Sunday. "Howdy, Guvnor."

Perhaps the imagination is the realm where the living and the dead conduct their transactions. If so, then we are in exile from that communion.

Except, perhaps, in dreams.

In a dream, for example, on my mother's last night on earth, her mother, Etta, appeared to me. No doubt the dream was so vivid because it took place downstairs, where I had been just before coming to bed. I had opened the back door for some reason and saw her in the darkened alley next to the house. She passed beneath a cone of light from a streetlamp. I was surprised but somehow not shocked that she was there. "Mammy Etta!" I said, very happy to see her. I had loved her very much as a child.

"Shhh." She put her finger to her lips then moved it back and forth. "I can't stay long," she whispered. She put her finger back to her lips and winked at me. And my mother died in the morning.

Or the dream I remembered while holding my grandson on my lap when he was five months old. I cupped his head in my hands, felt the lamb's-wool softness of his hair, nuzzled him, and looked in his eyes. A thrill, not a chill because it wasn't cold, a vibration of some kind went through me as I understood that I had dreamed of this child before he was born. My impulse was to shrug this off as déjà vu, a neurological glitch. However, I remembered that I had written about that dream because it puzzled me. Later, I went back to my journal to find it, prepared, by then, to laugh at myself for being so silly.

Such a strange dream last night. I'm in the backyard when a creature I don't recognize emerges from the bushes. It looks up at me with brown eyes, asking for something. It wants me to hold its head. I can't believe how soft and gentle it is. Its hair is soft as a lamb. I hold its cheeks in my hands, kiss its soft brown forehead. I am almost weeping with joy. What strange and beautiful creature is this?

The date of the entry is September 21, 2006, before we knew Veronica was pregnant, just around the time that D— my dreamt-of ancestor?—was conceived.

&

Neither Veronica nor I can recall whose idea it was, but I was the one who went to pick up the cake we had ordered for the family celebration of Kathi's successful treatment. I had never been in a bakery like this one before. In a glass display case were cookies and cakes in the shapes of penises, vaginas, sculptured cakes of copulating couples, weird armless and legless female torso cakes with shaved chocolate pubic hair. There was a little plate of bite-size pink penises with a sign above it: DELICIOUS—TRY ONE! There was a binder on the counter with pictures of all the other varieties of indelicate delicacies you could order.

"I'm here to pick up a cake," I said to the bald woman behind the counter.

"What's the name?"

"I think it's under Veronica." She went to a round-shouldered old refrigerator in the corner, took out a box, put it on the counter and opened it. "This it?"

The cake was in the shape of two round breasts, perfect domes with a nipple in the center of each one. Above them read, *Congratulations!* and below, *Super Woman!*

&

Recently, I was with my son, Robert, in the supermarket, just picking up a few items. There were only two registers in use and the lines were long, but there were several "self-serve" checkout machines free. I scanned my items and wished to pay with my debit card, but the correct menu wouldn't appear on the screen. Try again, I was prompted, twice. "Oh, for Christ's sake," I said. "You'd think if you were going to automate the process and put people out of work, you could at least get it right."

"Dad, hold on a minute."

"No, I'm serious." Now I was in a high working-class dudgeon. "There used to be seven or eight aisles here with cashiers and baggers. Where did those people go? Where'd those jobs go? Now you do the work yourself and they can't even keep their machines working right."

"Dad. Here. You have to touch the screen where it says debit."

I did. Then I was prompted to swipe my card and the rest of the transaction went off without a hitch. On our way out, I continued, "I just hate what those machines represent. There are so many people out of work. My first job was in a supermarket. How does a person get started now?" Robert put his hand on my shoulder.

"Okay, but still. I think we have to chalk this one up to user error. I don't disagree with you, but really, Dad, come on."

It's true that I've become impatient. I am gravely disappointed by my inability to stay young, and I am becoming more fully aware every day of the unlikelihood that I will outwit death and live forever. That small voice inside me that has all my life insisted on this special dispensation is now a child whose insistence that the world be different sometimes becomes a tantrum. All my many years have provided me is the wherewithal to come up with some articulate indictment of the world with which to express my abiding outrage. I answer the silent, powerful communique that is my son's hand on my shoulder in kind—with silence: mine is a fear he doesn't know yet. Besides, I do not want my foolish, tardy reckoning with reality to task my children, my friends, my students, with having to humor me. No fool like an old fool—and yet, though aging is not optional, becoming a fool is clearly the result of user error. My son drops his hand, I put my arm around him briefly and laugh. I believe we both understand what has just occurred.

&

It should get easier, going to see Damion, but it doesn't. For me, each time seems harder. Now I know how sad and angry I am going to feel afterward.

In front of Massachusetts Correctional Institution–Concord, beneath the Stars and Stripes, flies the black POW/MIA flag, even though it was determined years ago that the issue that it represents is bogus: Vietnam no longer has Americans imprisoned there. That whole idea, appealing to the grief and the hope of working people whose sons never returned, was birthed and exploited by Hollywood, specifically by Sylvester Stallone movies. Now, two decades later, it seems to me to be the perfect flag to hang outside a prison: a flag to stubbornness in the face of the facts, a flag that insists on an idea that has been repeatedly debunked.

There is a woman I see there in the waiting room no matter which day of the week I go. A white woman in her fifties, her hair dyed very black the way my mother wore hers, sitting with her hands crossed in her lap and legs crossed at her ankles. She smiles and says hello to other visitors. She's there to see her son. She comes every day, and every day she is smiling, as if, for her, this is not so much an impediment to her love but an inconvenience. I haven't yet decided if this is admirable or appalling.

When I'm here, I feel myself transformed into an object of scorn and pity. Or else I defiantly resist this transformation in a way that also disfigures me. I can hardly hold onto who I am in my own skin for half an hour. It's impossible to count all the tiny factors that undermine my sense of myself, but foremost is the attitude of the guards. Even when they are civil or polite, their faces betray their disdain. A few of the female guards will smile or make eye contact, but they are unpredictable and seem harder on female visitors, as if holding them responsible for being a bad influence or an insufficiently good one, for being a temptress or a shrew or a lousy mother. It is a kind of mud bath of shame, visiting this place.

This time I have come because Damion's father, Smithy, died of cancer two weeks earlier. Damion had not been allowed to attend his funeral in Connecticut. I knew from our earlier conversations that Damion's feelings for his father were as complicated as my own. I am happy for those men who feel no ambivalence, no confusion or puzzlement about their fathers. They are able either to follow their father's example or make a clean break and live unencumbered by the paternal ghost. I've never met a man like that, but they must exist somewhere.

As soon as he sits down, I tell him I'm sorry to hear about his father's death. He looks away, says nothing, shrugs. "He had a good life."

"You think so?"

"Better than this," he says, cocking his head to take in the whole room, the whole prison, maybe his whole life. "He got to do a lot. He went a lot of places. He got to do a lot of things he wanted to do."

I wait for him to go on, but when he doesn't I try to stick up for him. "I guess if I were you, among other things, I'd be mad. I guess I'm a little mad at him on your behalf."

"Nah. He was no kind of father. He just wasn't interested. I ain't going to judge him. I mean, that's the kind he was. That was just his way."

Then he tells me about an argument he got in with a guard.

"Is that why you couldn't go to your father's funeral?"

"Maybe. They said they didn't have nobody who could drive me down there. They couldn't spare a car that day."

Most people agree that what lands people in jail is either their poor choices or their lack of empathy for others. Our society, in its wisdom, has therefore chosen to create prison environments where regimentation eliminates choices—what time to rise and sleep, what to eat, what to wear, with whom to associate; and places in which empathy is not only unrewarded but is often an invitation to violence.

I ask him, again, to tell me what happened the night he was arrested.

"After I left the lawyer's I was like, I just want to spend time with my son. If I was going to jail on Monday, then I wanted the weekend with him. So I called Veronica. You know that part."

I do. And as I sit there, the two of us sitting forward, elbows on our knees, being as honest as we can, I'm thinking of all the ways this could have turned out to be even more tragic. "What if she'd agreed? What if she'd relaxed the rule?"

"What do you mean?"

"I mean then D would have been with you in that car, with you and your friends."

"No, man! No. It wasn't like that. If I'd had D with me, I would have been at my aunt's house. I would never have been with those guys." He leans back, looks at me as if he's trying to decide whether to be insulted. He shakes his head. "It wasn't like that."

I believe him.

He went over to a friend's house in the projects, where they sat around drinking beer and watching TV for a while, waiting for another friend who never showed. He was the only one with a car, so when it got late he offered to give the other three guys a ride home. They had just piled in and Damion had just started the car when an unmarked police car pulled in front of him and blocked the way. These cops, known as the gang task force, were notorious for riding herd on young men in the projects.

"They told us to get out of the car. And I was like, 'We ain't doing nothing wrong. I know my rights. Why don't you move your damn car and let me get up out of here?' But the dudes in the back seat, they got out the car and on a count of three, they ran in all kind of directions. The cop slammed me on the car and stuck his elbow in my back. I wasn't running or trying to get away but he did it again. I told him, 'Don't do that!' When he did it again, I turned and caught him with my elbow. That's when he hit me in the mouth with his flashlight and busted my tooth."

He ran but he didn't get very far. In the backseat, along with two guns on the floor, his friends had left a bag containing several handguns and a couple of Kevlar vests. Damion insists he knew nothing about them.

I want to believe him. I don't care as much about whether he knew anything about the guns in the backseat as I do about whether he is lying to me. I want to believe that he tells me the truth.

In a recent letter, he writes, "There's no feeling worse than that of being cheated out of life. Being a man, you always have to take responsibility for your own actions. So I accept what happened as a consequence of my own actions."

But to what extent is that the truth? I want to object; I want to remind him that from the moment he arrived here from Jamaica as a boy, he was marked by the darkness of his skin and the fears of those who still frantically roll up their windows, who would spit him out if they could. Once he told me that he didn't know he was black until he came to the United States, and that for a time he corrected people who called him that. "No, I'm sorry. I'm from Jamaica."

Am I letting him off the hook? But it's none of it fair: when in his entire young life has he not been *on the hook*? I recognize that his acceptance of accountability is a load-bearing wall of his self-respect, so I keep my mouth shut, but I don't accept such a privatization of responsibility, either. The whole world must be "buyer beware"? Every man for himself? All he can do now is try to use the time to grow up. Is prison a place where one can do that? I wonder.

&

One last thing about the film *Attack!* While I wouldn't call it an antiwar movie as we have come to know that genre, it is clear throughout that none of the soldiers wants to be in combat. They are no longer raw recruits. They have left friends dead in the field. We hear the groans and cries of the wounded. When it appears that they will not be sent to "the show" again, they are relieved.

Attack! is a film about courage and honor. It is clearly on the side of the enlisted man. The real antagonist is not the Third Reich, but their cowardly Captain Cooney, who twice refuses to come to the aid of Costa's men, resulting in needless lives lost to his cowardice. The other officer, a colonel played by Lee Marvin, is a friend of Cooney's father, a judge, and his postwar political ambitions determine his every move, including retaining Cooney in command of the unit even though he knows he is weak and unsuited to the job. After Cooney's second betrayal, and while the Germans are advancing in increased numbers, the plot revolves around Costa's promise to hunt down Cooney and avenge his men. The moral quandary faced by the other appealing character in the film, Costa's friend Harry, who is Cooney's adjutant, is about either adhering to the army's code of conduct or turning a blind eye to Costa's fragging. In the end, after Costa's death, it is Harry who kills Cooney. Then in a final scene, the code of conduct coming back to the fore, he calls command to report what he has done.

It is a complicated plot, all of which I'm sure was lost on me as a child. Costa's platoon contains a Jewish soldier, Bernstein, whose wisecracking does much to keep up morale. When he is wounded and Nazis are about to overrun their position, they decide to stay and fight: "These guys are SS, Lieutenant, you know that we can't leave Bernstein here." I would not even have asked why this would be so. A good portion of childhood's innocence is simple ignorance.

What I'm sure was also lost on me but would nevertheless have made an impression, was that there were no women in the film, none. There is a woman's voice on the radio early in the film, from Armed Forces Radio, seductive and encouraging to the soldiers, but there are no women on the roads, in the villages, in the countryside. There are no civilians; everyone in the film is in uniform.

And so I am five, and I'm holding on to my father's thumb. We are on our way back home from the movies. Because I am shaky and weak and confused, I will watch my father; work to assimilate his walk, his mannerisms, his attitudes. I have somehow forgotten how it is to be me. When we left home I was a child; now I am a boy, and I will school myself in the world of my father, a world of heroes and cowards, of honor and dishonor, a world with no women, where men must contend with other men to stay alive.

Part Three

The real man, whoever he had been,
had suffered and now was dead:
this was all that was sure and all that
mattered now. Every man in the chapel
hoped that when his hour came he, too,
would be eulogized, which is to say
forgiven, and that all of his lapses,
greeds, errors, and strayings from the
truth would be invested with coherence
and looked upon with charity.

JAMES BALDWIN

W hat the hell is Henry doing?" Joe asks me. My cousin Margaret's husband is walking all around my father's casket, shooting pictures. At one point, leaning over the bier, he stumbles, recovers, knocks a flower from a bouquet. He tries to stand on the padded kneeler to get a little more height so he can take a shot looking down at my father's face but thinks better of it.

"He just got a new camera."

Earlier, in the hall, I'd seen him down on one knee, taking a shot of the placard on an easel with my father's name. Across the hall, someone else's name in an elegant script. Henry showed me a picture he'd taken of the outside of the funeral home. "The trick with digital is to try all different settings. You don't have to worry about using up film. And you want to shoot from as many angles as you can. Look, look here, with the digital zoom I can zoom in even after I've taken the picture."

"He wants to shoot from different angles," I tell my brother.

"Yeah, but what the hell is he *doing?*"

Joe and I are standing next to each other off to the side of where the folding chairs are arranged for the mourners who have just begun arriving. My son, Robert, has joined us and stands to my right. Kathi and Veronica are in the first row of chairs with D, only days past his first birthday, on Veronica's lap. It is a moment of calm after all the necessary inanities about caskets and vaults, talk of waterproofing, of warranties and reinforcements so the grave will not cave in, of how many limos will roll slowly through the streets to the cemetery, all our delusional begrudging the earth what it rightfully owns.

Shoulder to shoulder with my brother, I am thinking about our different engagements with our father. For decades mine was long distance, made of phone calls, holiday visits, and scripted versions of my life usually more true than not but always wary and defensive. My brother, on the other hand, lived all those years in that dark house, the curtains drawn, our father in his chair sinking ever deeper into an irascible depression. Somehow, for his psychic survival, Joe managed to distance himself as surely as I had by remaining hundreds of miles away. And yet we loved the man, each of us.

Standing there, the brother who left, next to the brother who stayed, I find myself wondering where it is written that a son must be dutiful and obedient, must sacrifice himself for his father's love, its expression withheld and replaced by a promise, an assurance that is unfelt and unseen?

Above my father in the casket, a crucifix hangs midair, suspended by invisible wire, as if presiding over the arrangements of flowers and the gathering mourners.

Only weeks before, as we sat before his gigantic television, my father had made his wishes known. He pressed the mute button on the remote. "I hope it will be okay with you and your brother, but I've decided not to have a funeral Mass in the church."

"Okay? You know me. I think 99 percent of religions give all the others a bad name."

He gave me a disgusted look as if to say that this was no time to be cute.

"I just don't want to be a hypocrite," he said. "I stopped going to Mass a long time ago. I think Joe still goes, maybe Christmas and Easter, so he might feel strongly about it. . . ."

"It doesn't matter to me."

"Well, then, unless your brother objects, I'd just as soon have the priest just come over to the funeral home and say a rosary or something." He jabbed the remote at the TV and *SportsCenter* drowned out any further talk.

In the dream I had the night before the funeral, I had written the story of my life, and my father, like a circus strongman tearing a phone book, ripped it in half, then in half again, and yet again until he scattered the pieces to the wind like confetti. He was calm, not enraged, undisturbed, as if to say, "So, what else have you got?" The dream was too transparent, even to me, asleep, to be a nightmare so I didn't feel terror, only a kind of resignation, a sigh: Oh, not *again*. I even wondered, in the dream, why I gave him the story to read, knowing what he would likely do. But who was this dream father, really? Surely not the man who worked to bend his desires to his obligations; who sacrificed, loved, grieved, and survived; not the man who, confronted with his failures, determined to set things right; not the man who we were grieving here today.

And yet that same man could be a monster, a wanton agent of psychic destruction. My brother told me a story once that should have made me angry on his behalf but only chilled me to the bone and left me grateful once again that I left home when I did. Joe had been working in those days for the local chapter of the Nature Conservancy, and he'd been asked to give a talk on the preservation of a waterway in a neighboring township. Our father had been watching TV, of course, and, surfing channels, discovered my brother's presentation on the local station.

"Hey, you never told me you were going to be on my television!" he said while my brother was hanging up his jacket. "I sat here and thought, This is a damn good speech. This guy sounds like he really knows what he's talking about!"

"Thanks. Thanks a lot," Joe said, a little wary. "Glad you thought so."

"You know, it's too bad the way you look. People would pay more attention to what you say if you just weren't so fuckin' ugly."

"What did you do when he said that?" I asked Joe.

"I went upstairs to my room. What the hell else could I do?"

I could see him, anger shaking him, pulling himself up the bannister, climbing the stairs deliberately, and closing, not slamming, his bedroom door. I'd witnessed our father shaming him before, many times. And I hadn't done a damn thing.

Another time, when my brother was dating a young Korean woman, he mused, resigned, "What am I going to do, bring her home so he can ask her, 'Now, just what kind of a gook are you, exactly?'" I wanted to say that he could move out, but somehow, for some reason I can't understand, that wasn't true.

Once I told a therapist that it seemed to me my father must have given me my sense of myself as competent and resilient. I was thinking of my mother's unworldliness and insecurity. He asked me if it wasn't more likely that my father had not succeeded in taking that confidence away from me. Now I have come to think that I made my escape before he could do that, before he could finish the job.

My brother and I, of course, each had our own relationship to our father. We're talking here about love, after all, not sociology. Grief has always seemed to me to be love made briefly visible, like a crackling tree of lightning forking across the night sky. But that glimpse of love's ramifying light, all its meanings in a single instant, vanishes, and all you're left with is the knowledge that more things are connected to one another and in more eccentric and surprising ways than you can possibly trace. Maybe in his way this is what Henry is trying to capture. Maybe it is what I was doing staring at my father naked on a rusty gurney.

Maybe I am trying to fix that lightning, or at least the memory of it, here, in these words.

Arrangements of flowers surround the casket, and there is no other way to approach, to come close to my father this last time, except to kneel. And so I kneel beneath that molded figure of agony twisted in the same pose as a billion others, stamped out like so many pennies, and I am shaking like a man with Parkinson's, wanting to feel something coherent and simple and untangled. I can't.

I stare at my father's hands that fed me and struck me, teaching me gratitude and terror. I recall a time he threw me against a wall so hard my head snapped back and I lost consciousness, coming to with a touch of nausea and a taste in the back of my throat like nothing else. And then my father shined his flashlight in my eyes to watch my pupils respond, his hand steadying my chin—"Keep still, damn it!"—his look as if searching in my soul for something. "You'll be okay," he said, switching off the light.

Entwined in his fingers, a rosary. Who had requested that? I feel an invitation to anger on his behalf; what did his being Catholic ever afford him but shame? And yet it doesn't matter. It's a bit of tribal superstition, a vestige of Catholic exceptionalism, packing off the deceased with the means to prove he was of the one true church, but it would no doubt comfort some of the people who'd come and, other than me, it was likely to offend no one.

I want to reach into the casket and touch his hands but I know how icy they will be. His left is crossed over his right, his thumb perfectly the shape of mine, at precisely the same angle to the rest of the hand. And suddenly I want to thank my father for my thumb. It clearly came from him, or through him, and science would say it is the most important tool he left me, more important than his whole red metal box of tools with its trays and drawers, its wrench with a socket for every occasion, its place for everything and everything in its place. But this is not just any thumb, no. It's plain as day to me that whatever my mother left me of all that I am, this thumb came from him: same shape; same angle, exactly; same size relative to my hand. I don't mean to suggest that my father's thumb was odd or remarkable, only that I, his firstborn son, know the lineaments, texture, movements of that thumb that I could never mistake for another. I probably watched that thumb holding a baby bottle in the middle of my first ferocious hungers when, as my mother told me, he walked the floor with me night after colicky night. Buckling buckles, tying my shoes, cutting up my food. And, some furious years later, pressing on my Adam's apple, his hand around my neck. And telling me to hit the road. I know that thumb. This thumb.

Then Henry's kneeling next to me. "Here, look at this one," he says, and he shows me the screen of his camera where I am in focus, kneeling there, my father's face a little blurry in the background. He understands the look I give him: "Sorry. I'll leave you alone." Then he whispers, "I'll save this one for you. This is a good one." As Henry leaves, my father's face seems a comment, a bemused, "Yup. That's Henry."

I'm still trembling, not yet ready to rise. I feel certain there is something here I am supposed to understand. I want to mourn my father, mourn him and be done with it, mourn him and be done with him. But the contradictions pull at me, twist me. I am grateful and outraged, sorrowful and relieved. The judgments, the recriminations, the guilt, the anger all get in my way. And the questions. I am still trying to know him, still asking who he was, unable to make even my own experience of him cohere.

Or maybe this is just my reluctance to let him go. Who, after all, has a continuous sensible experience of oneself? It's more like a passage we must make through the dark, underground, with a miner's lamp on our helmets: at any given moment we can only see a little part of where we are.

I have to admit he was more comfortable with his many contradictions than I am with mine. I am always trying to make sense, doing a kind of corrective surgery on myself. Is this striving for coherence a disguise for narcissism? I hear my father's voice, "What are you bucking for, sainthood?" I was a kid in Catholic school when he first made that crack. I don't remember the occasion, but I recall thinking, why not? What else is worth aiming for? Now I hear a world-weary wisdom in his remark and a warning against a certain spiritual arrogance.

My father was raised in a German family, in a Prussian culture, in fact, the son of a coal miner and an Irish Catholic daughter of the Great Hunger. He grew up in the Great Depression, left school for the army, and when the war was over, he married my mother and attempted to begin a life that would make some sense, that would be orderly and satisfying and good. For a few years it was. I was born first, then my brother Bobby. Soon Bobby was sick. Joe was born. Mike was born. Bobby and Mike were diagnosed with muscular dystrophy. Life became hardship, the daily struggle against despair and cynicism. That struggle never seemed to take place in any kind of way he could articulate. He had no vocabulary except the harsh Catholicism he was raised with and which he walked away from (farther after each death, for which it offered him neither comfort nor consolation), so that by the end of his life he was left shuffling fourteen kinds of pills to try to manage his moods, his digestion, his energy, his appetite, his sleep. It was all he could do to survive. Why insist on coherence with courage in such supply? My father does not have to be understood, or even be understandable, for me to have loved him all my life and to love him still.

And to remain furious with him.

Why is it that when I let the anger kick in the tears finally come? Somebody says to me, "Come on, come on. They want to get this show on the road." It can't have been my father. I did hear it though, in his voice, complete with his impatience, right in the middle of my head.

And as I rise from the kneeler, glancing up at the crucifix, I cross myself before I know what I'm doing, my body reminding me it doesn't need my permission to remember.

When I return and stand between my brother and my son, Robert touches me on the shoulder, and I need my handkerchief. I've just about got things back under control when I feel D collide with my leg and wrap his arms around it tight. When I look down at him, at his one-year-old face, I see empathy, spontaneous, instinctual. I pick him up and kiss him and he squirms to go back to Veronica.

The undertaker directs the people who have been filing

in, sitting in folding chairs. Joined by some who have been waiting in the hall, they form a line to pay their last respects to my father, and then to express their sorrow to my brother and me, and to Kathi and the kids. Singly or in twos, they make their way to the bier and kneel a few moments. Some of them look at my father's face, some cross themselves as they rise.

At first I was surprised at how few of my father's old pals were at his funeral. I thought I might see Eddie, who ran the newsstand at Sixth and Turner streets where I picked up my bundle of evening newspapers for my afternoon route; rows and rows of colorful magazines, and newspapers not only from out of town, but from several countries represented in the immigrant population of the city. There were publications in Spanish, German, Polish, Greek. I thought that Eddie must be very smart to be able to read all those different languages, but my father set me straight. "Don't be fooled. He only sells those things. He don't read them. Eddie's an old prizefighter. I'd be careful of him. He's a good guy but a little punchy." And I remember there was a section close to the cash register where the magazines were covered in brown paper.

Or Tooty, the groundskeeper at Irving Street Park, where the infield was smooth and level as a clay tennis court and the outfield was like a putting green. Or Schmidty, assistant coach of my father's American Legion team, for which I'd been the batboy.

But of course, it dawned on me, they were all dead. My father, with his many griefs, who had buried two sons and his wife, who had been angry, abidingly angry every day of his life, who had lived to know his grandchildren and meet his great-grandson, had survived them. I felt a foolish momentary pride I knew better than to take to heart.

My father preferred the company of men. He felt that he understood men. In fact, it would have been impossible for him, in his time and place, class and circumstance, to have ever been friends with a woman. My own coming-of-age coincided with the rise of second-wave feminism, and my friendships with women have been a crucial part of my life. Once, I mentioned to my father that I was having dinner with my friend Suzanne, a fellow writer, and frowning he asked, "Does Kathi know about this?"

Most of the people who approach us to express sympathy are strangers to me. My brother Joe knows a good number of them, but many are people my father worked with in the years after I left Allentown.

Will, as close to my father as either of his sons, is here from Michigan. He gives my hand a squeeze, looks down, shakes his head. "You were right. Remember what you told me on the phone? The world is different now." Will once told me that my father found me a mystery. "How's a kid leave home a quarterback and come back a poet?" Will, with his PhD in literature, must have seemed to my father the only person he could ask such a question. He didn't say how he'd answered.

There's a large open area between the bier and the rows of chairs, and D is racing back and forth across it, Veronica running behind, scooping him up, putting him back down, redirecting him as much as possible. She has been crying, her eyes red, a wad of tissues in her hand, but she has to laugh despite that. So do several other of the mourners. Now D, dressed in a suit with a clip-on tie, pants big enough for his diaper, decides to run in a circle. He seems to have just figured out, or is delighting in the fact, that if he runs in a circle away from his mother and she stays put he will soon come back to her. Every time he slams back into her she

picks him up and kisses him. The next time he takes off, Veronica gets down on one knee, ready to receive him when he
comes back, but D takes that as a new wrinkle in the game:
he teases her and then runs off in another direction, out into
the hall, where his mother chases after him. Except for a few
stern souls, people are smiling, wiping their eyes, blowing
their noses perhaps, but then smiling. I wonder at him. How
will he fare without his father, now in a cell awaiting trial?
How will he fare at all? I wonder in both joy and fear: who
will he become? And will it matter who he is, or only how
the white world sees him?

"I'm Bill Dolan. Your dad got me a job driving a mower
in the parks in the summers when I was home from college. I'd sometimes see him around. He was one of the good
guys." I recognize Dolan as a guy I knew in high school. He
was a senior who played varsity football when I was on the
freshman team, so he doesn't remember me.

My cousin Don, here with his young family, shakes my
hand. I recall my Aunt Marietta's chagrin when he became
a Jehovah's Witness. "There's no Christmas or nothing," she
complained. "I can't even make him a birthday cake!"

"Wow. Donnie. It's been a long time." I know the weight
he carries: a father, my Uncle Pete, who drank himself to
death, and I feel the urge to connect with him somehow.
"We should get together sometime. Some other time, I
mean." But I know as I say it that it won't happen. He gives
me his card. He owns a car dealership. "I'll shoot you an
e-mail," I tell him.

A man is shaking Joe's hand next to me, and I hear him
say, " . . . A long time ago, at the Boys Club." A short, stout
African American man, hair going to gray, he steps up to
me, takes my hand in both of his, says, "I'm sorry for your
loss," and moves away. A member of the hambone team? I

am staring after him, wondering, when a soft clear voice says, "Richard."

She is standing in front of me, radiant and tall although she must be in her eighties. She takes my hand. "I'm Mrs. McFadden."

"Of course," I manage to say, "yes, yes of course," though history has just now rung me like a bell. She is my childhood friend Patrick's mother. Patrick was the oldest of, I believe, eleven or twelve kids. I remember only two of his siblings, Rosemary and Timmy, probably because they were old enough to play with us. I remember the house always smelled of ammonia from a diaper pail, which after five minutes you didn't notice anymore, and Mrs. McFadden was almost continuously pregnant, with one child on her hip and another by the hand as she calmly answered our questions or told us what she wanted Patrick and me to pick up for her at the corner store. My other friends' mothers were tolerant, at least if it was raining; otherwise they chased us outside to play. Mrs. McFadden seemed happy I was there. I don't think I ever knew what Mr. McFadden did, but I remember that when there were nine McFadden kids, my father declared that now there were enough for a baseball team. A couple of years later he said there were enough for a football team. Once, when I was in high school, my father asked me what Patrick's father did, and I shrugged. I didn't care much about things like that, and in those days I didn't care much for my father. "Well, he's got eleven kids," my father said, "so I know one thing he's doing for shit-sure!"

"This is my son, Robert." She smiles broadly. "And that's my daughter, Veronica, whose been chasing my grandson around here. And my wife Kathi's there in the first row." She looks back at Robert. "He looks like his mother," she says to me. "Do people tell you that, Robert? That you look like your mother?"

I haven't seen this woman for decades; I might pass her on the street without stopping, but now I feel an affection so vast it summons another place and time. I am in the old neighborhood, in St. Francis of Assisi Parish, North Ninth Street running uptown to the public library and department stores and in the other direction ending in three glorious sledding hills declining to the freight siding and scrap metal yards of Sumner Avenue. Across town my uncle is under another chassis at Mack Trucks, welding; my mother is taking her tuna casserole from the oven, checking to see if she has time to run to Woodring's grocery, where big Jim in his butcher's apron would write down what she spent in a thick ledger—"Put it on the bill," my mother would say to him—but no, the boys will be traipsing in wanting something to eat in fifteen or twenty minutes, so she can ask me to go for her then; Aunt Helen is in between customers at the diner, smoking in back and wondering if she might take off her shoes to ease her swollen feet or if she'd better not because she wouldn't be able to get them on again; the public school kids are already out, a half hour earlier than us; along the south side of town trout see the surface of the Little Lehigh dimple with the first drops of rain. Mrs. Dries's Doberman paces back and forth, looking pissed off that nobody has come by to terrify by snarling on his hind legs at the gate; traffic on Seventh Street circles the city's Soldiers and Sailors monument, Nike, goddess of victory atop a ninety-foot marble pillar; my father is working at the brewery, grabbing longneck bottles of beer by the top, four at a time, off the conveyor belt—six times per case—laughing with his co-worker Stanley; a few guys, out of work, are playing basketball at the Salvation Army court, where if you drive through the key and fall into the heavy doors you might go through and right down the steps; my grandmother starts out on her walk, six blocks from her apartment to our house in time to help my mother set the table; at my desk I'm watching the clock, which is next to the crucifix and above the twenty-six letters of the alphabet; Johnny Pacheco is, of course, in trouble again and the nun has him by the ear but he is grinning at us as she drags him away; the Royal laundry truck Ronnie's father drives backs up to the platform for its final load of the day; the birds gather on wires above Freihofer's bakery, in winter for the warmth coming out of the stacks from the ovens, and all year round for whatever crumbs might become available.

"Are you still on Ninth Street?"

"Oh, yes."

"How is the neighborhood?"

"Oh, it's about the same. All the old people are gone, but the new neighbors are nice. There are lots of children. Everyone speaks Spanish, though, and I don't understand a word they say. Well, it's lovely to see you, Richard; I'm very sorry for your loss."

My cousin Margaret approaches me. She has her purse open, and I think she is going to offer me a tissue, but she takes out a compact. "I figured I should ask you first. Would it be okay if I just put a little rouge on him? They left him looking awfully pale." I dissuade her. She leans in closer, a look of aggravation on her face, and whispers, "Did they let you pick out a casket?"

"Why? You don't like it?" She pats my hand, dabs at her eyes, and moves away.

When all of the people are seated, the priest enters. Joe knows him. Father Marty, his name is. Already I feel the tone is off; it is a solemn occasion, after all, a man's funeral, even if he preferred that things be kept simple. Father Marty seemed to bop in, bouncing on the balls of his feet, rubbing his hands together as if he were about to organize a picnic. He makes a brief stop at the bier, kneeling for a moment to whisper a prayer; he crosses himself as he rises. He comes forward and intones a blessing, crossing the air in front of him. "In the name of the Father, and of the Son, and of the Holy Spirit." Only a scattering of people respond, "Amen."

He's trying. I have some sympathy for him. He didn't know my father. He's sticking to the tried and true, to generalities he must have been taught in his coursework in pastoral care. He is facing a motley flock here: in addition to my Catholic cousins—varying from devout to lapsed—the room includes many Lutherans, at least one Buddhist, two Jehovah's Witnesses, several Jews, a Unitarian, and a number of atheists. If he is aware of this fact, he's not letting it impede his ministrations.

When I was a young altar boy, sometimes the priest would come into our classroom, sixth or seventh grade, whisper something to the nun, and she would point to me and to one of the other altar boys, maybe Patrick, maybe Peter. And we would join Father Walters in the hall, where he would explain that there was to be a funeral Mass this afternoon and that we had been chosen to serve. I remember my first time, carrying a candle around the casket as the priest, just behind me, swung the censor—*chingchingching* . . . *chingchingching*—and I heard the weeping, a wail here and there, and saw the wet, red faces of the mourners and could not completely keep from crying myself. I can remember the scratchy rayon of my black cassock on my cheek as I tried to wipe away a tear. But I came to see, as I served at more funerals, a certain purity in the contorted faces of the grieving, a concentration of emotion, something so sincere that I felt deeply reassured. It was like seeing straight into a white light, the acetylene center of the soul, where all the colors meet, fuse, transcend distinctions. Later on, at the funerals of my own family members, I found this reassurance again, that we are all connected by grief to everyone else in the human web: a net, after all, is made of crosses. But there's not sufficient comfort in transcendent understandings. We grieve, we mourn; we do not shrug. To survive the death of a loved one is to have withstood, somehow, all the sorrow of our species passing through us in a particular moment, like a dense speck of negative light, one of those imploded stars astronomers tell us change the universe forever.

negative light — ?

I can hear D in the hall, crying because his mother has picked him up, restraining him a bit, maybe to keep him from toddling into the funeral across the hall, but in my present state of mind I hear him grieving, too, complaining of the weight on him, the burdens he never asked for tumbling down the generations, his early and wordless apprehension of the way things are. I hear confusion and defiance; I hear the demand for an explanation, the need for comfort.

Father Marty is giving it his best shot with what he's been given to work with: only moments earlier I saw the funeral director whispering in his ear. When he says, "Beloved of many, many others, besides those who are here today," I halfway think he is commenting on the paucity of those present. He acknowledges "the deceased's sons and grandson," bowing slightly in our direction, but neglects to mention Veronica, an omission that doesn't escape Kathi's notice. After a quarter-century of marriage, we have a rich lexicon of nuanced aspect and expression, and she gives me a look that tells me that she is thinking what I think she is thinking: that it is a not unforgiveable but nevertheless maddeningly predictable oversight from an officer of the world's oldest boys' club.

My marriage to Kathi was the site of my fiercest battles with myself, disguised for a time as a battle with the alcohol that kept the whole rickety structure of what I thought of as myself in soft, or at least intermittent, focus.

I loved her. She loved me. But not only did neither of us feel much joy in that fact, neither of us felt any confidence that we could keep the marriage. We tried couples counseling, and more than once. At a difficult moment in one session, the two of us in separate chairs, the therapist completing the triad, I cried out in frustration: "Jesus Christ, why don't we just get your mother and my father in here and let them duke it out?"

The therapist, an engaged and demonstrative psychologist, threw up her hands, pitched forward in her chair and flung her long hair in a veil over her face. We stopped. Silence. Then she sat up, parted the curtain of hair before her face, sighed, and said, "Richard, for God's sake, what do you think we've been doing all this time?"

Now I think it more that I wish we could have had *my* mother and father in that room, and that we could have brokered and judged *that* argument. In fact, back then I was still grieving my mother, dead less than two years, whose granddaughter, whom she would never meet, had just been born.

Kathi and my father weren't close. Neither disliked the other. Each was admiring—Kathi of my father's resilience and fortitude, my father of Kathi's accomplishments, intelligence, and practicality. Neither especially enjoyed the other's company, however. No one knew better than Kathi the injuries, fears, and incapacities my father had bequeathed me, but she also saw him as a man who always meant to do the right thing.

I could never talk with my father about my marriage. I did not rely on him to have any wisdom to offer. I'd seen my parents' marriage crumble under extraordinary pressure of circumstance, devolve into a kind of "toughing it out." And yet, during the time when it seemed our marriage was coming apart, he surprised me when I told him we weren't doing well. "Just remember, you're not an easy guy to live with. You're not. Keep that in mind."

"Let us recite the prayer that Jesus taught us," Father Marty instructed. "Our Father . . ."

The murmur of the recitation seemed to calm D in Veronica's arms with his thumb in his mouth. The words were on my lips but they stayed there.

What are we called these days, those of us who have left the church? Are we *lapsed? Failed? Fallen?* I suppose we are officially apostates, but what does that really mean? I guess that depends on where you stand, or kneel, or if you have to keep your unbelief quiet: maybe you're a florist or an undertaker or a church architect or that other guy, the sexton, who keeps the gold all shiny and the floors buffed and the wood polished, along with who knows how many other people who have reasons good and not so good all mashed together to keep them, at least nominally, Catholic. Only they know if they should also be counted in the roll of the lapsed, the apostate. Or are we the fallen, like the angels Michael threw out of heaven. *Non serviam.*

When I was a kid you couldn't eat for twelve hours before communion, a long, long time when you're a child. You're eight or nine years old, able to take communion now because after the age of seven, the "age of reason," you are responsible for your own soul, no excuses. You went to bed the night before, hungry, without your usual bedtime snack of bread and butter or peanut butter crackers, starving as only a kid can be starving, with only a rosary and you can't eat that. After a while, your stomach seeming to join you in the Hail Marys, you wonder what all those little yellow circles are floating around your room, and you finally decide they are the eyes of the many angels, drawn to your praying, flying through your room like those transparent tropical fish swimming in their tank at the pet store, just about invisible except for their bulging eyes. You can see them, the angels, only on those nights before you are going to communion. You take this as proof that you are holy in your post-confessional state of grace, and you would explain, if anyone asked, that the reason that their eyes were the only part of the fishy angels you could see was that the seeing, the looking, the taking it all in from as many angles as possible, is what we have in common with the angels, not our stupid thoughts that can't even figure simple math, remember the times tables, the infield fly rule, or the differences between the ways the apostles were martyred.

Sometimes turning things over and over, looking from different angles, can even trick you into thinking you're just like Jesus: God's son, not your father's. But that is a terrible thought, a sinful thought, and you have to chase it away at once, this pride. Now you'll have to stay awake longer, praying for forgiveness so you can still be in a state of grace in case you die in your sleep. You're hungry, scared that you've sinned, ashamed and begging forgiveness, but the fishy angels are still swimming round you, so you must be still okay.

Next morning, at a Solemn High Mass, the incense gets to you. They even teach you, if you're an altar boy, how to loop the chains over your fingers and let the burner—the thurible!, and what a great word to learn—hang down so you can swing it back and forth with just a little finger action like a puppeteer and pump out clouds of sweet smoke that on an empty stomach can take you out—bam!—just like that. One of the older boys warns you that when that happens you could piss your pants or even shit yourself because when you faint you have no control over that. So you make sure you go before you leave for Mass. You are learning your religion with your body. In church, you're supposed to kneel up straight unless you're old or fat; then you can rest your wide behind on the bench behind you. Everybody's stomach is making sounds like squeaky hinges or wet feet in sneakers, and then finally it's time.

When you go up to the altar rail you get to the front of the aisle and stand there and wait until someone gets up so you can take their spot that the priest has already passed. You look to see if this is the priest who works his way back along the rail in the other direction or if this is the one who turns and marches back to the place he started from with the altar boy hurrying behind him. Soon he's there and you close your eyes—unless the altar boy is a friend of yours who might try to use the edge of the gold-plated paddle (the paten, pronounced like the general) to deal a quick blow to your Adam's apple. So you stick out your tongue, and this thinnest wafer of bread that wasn't hardly bread to begin with and now isn't bread at all but the body and blood of Our Lord and Savior Jesus Christ lands on your tongue and all the juices suddenly flow. Sometimes your mouth stings then, and for all you want to sink your teeth into this thin chip of God, you dare not. On your way back to your pew, the Lord melts in your mouth. He tells you, as you look as holy for your parents as you can manage, that He's going to save you, your blood sugar rising now, just enough to keep you conscious till you get home and eat a bowl of cornflakes. Along the side of a house I once lived in, every summer tall fleshy bamboolike weeds sprung up. They stank and they had a nacreous milky sap in their hollow stalks that was hard to scrub from your hands. Over and over I yanked each stalk up from the ground by what seemed to be the roots—they dangled, dribbling clods—but they were really a kind of camouflage or trick. In fact, underground there was a long rope of a root, a rhizome, that stretched the length of the house and beyond and mocked my every effort.

I may as well give in and acknowledge a certain hunger for symmetry that feels like the distilled essence of my freighted and shame-crooked childhood faith.

The expression is "Once a Catholic, always a Catholic." I am forever running into certain loops and knots in my thinking that suggest my hard drive has been formatted a certain way, with a Catholic operating system installed. If honesty is the antidote to all that smoky mumbo jumbo, then it begins with an acknowledgment of how at odds with yourself it leaves you to have turned away from it—ah, there! Turned away. I'm a *turned away* Catholic. Perfect. It is impossible to tell if *I* turned away, in the sense of repudiating the past, or was turned away like a guy at a restaurant without a jacket and tie. And that's, honestly, the truth: I'm not sure myself.

I'm left with tribal scars, axioms inscribed on the body, deep in the cortex from which ideas arise. I have long dismissed my yearning as mere nostalgia for the "smells, bells, and spells" of the Latin mass, and it is that, but also so much more. I am a captive of these first premises, the starting point for my consciousness, the cardinal directions making any map, and any journey at all, possible in the first place.

I once called myself an estranged Catholic. Asked why

I'd left the Church, I replied that the Church had left me, that it had taken a hard right turn and kept on going where I couldn't, in conscience, follow. This is at least partly true.

There's a torn place, a jagged space between the faith that remains mine and the beliefs that made it all so seamless and comfortable. That space fills, now, with yearning. It is why my eyes well up whenever I listen to the chanting, the prayers, the several missae of Bach, Mozart, Lassus, Vivaldi, Palestrina, and others. Those tears may be the real fruit of my Catholic acculturation—now doctrineless or at least heterodox to the point of bewilderment—I'm left with sadness, wonder, compassion for myself and others, all of us doing what we can to understand how we came into being, where we're going, if we're going anywhere at all, whether life is what it seems, or more, or even denying, refusing, rejecting those questions.

Mainly, I am left with the unshakable conviction that life is a moral contest that will be judged at the hour of my death. I say unshakable because I know: I have tried to shake it off like a dog emerging from a lake. I have rolled on harsh ground, writhed against rough bark, all the while looking rabid and dangerous to those who find the idea of such a *Dies Irae* an embarrassing superstition in one they otherwise took to be an intelligent, rational person. But for myself, having tried to excise this expectation of a reckoning and finding it safely lodged out of reach deep in my own heart, I'm about as content as I believe a human being can ever be: I choose from among first principles what is already mine. As a man must eat and breathe, I accept what I require.

Is there such a thing as a post-Catholic Catholic?

"I keep a separate Sabbath," as the poet said. Often I go into Catholic churches and sit in that quiet with the scent of incense, the shimmering tiered trays of votive lights. I sit. I do not kneel. I do not genuflect and cross myself as I was taught to do. The holy water in the fonts is not for me, has not been for me for more than four decades. I remind myself that I am not superior to those who light tapers and kneel (slipping a dollar in the slot.) But I have to remind myself, and I am humbled, shamed, by that knowledge of my own pharisaical pride.

I tell myself I am admiring the architecture, the art, the ways that the stained-glass panels form a narrative, the sculpted bas-reliefs of the Stations of the Cross on the walls, the craftsmanship; but for better and for worse the stamp of this belief system, its culture, its aesthetic and ethical precepts, is on this helpless soul forever.

Henry is circling Father Marty, his camera making a soft whirring sound as he shoots him over and over again.

At the end of the Lord's Prayer, when some of the assembled have veered down the Protestant road: *For Thine is the kingdom, and the power, and the glory . . .* trailing off when they realize they are fewer voices than before, Father Marty segues to a hymn, "Love Divine, All Loves Excelling." Two, maybe three of my cousins, Aunt Kitty's daughters, know it and join in, along with Mrs. McFadden and one or two others.

Love Divine, all loves excelling,
Joy of heaven, to earth come down

Father Marty, singing loudly, gestures with his arms, coaxing. He moves closer to the assembled and strides across the front of the area to appeal to others who are not singing. "Everybody!" he says.

Fix in us thy humble dwelling

I might sing, just to join in and because I love to sing, but I don't know the words. Father Marty is moving back across the front in a semicrouch, palms up, singing even louder, wheeling his arms as if exhorting everyone to scoop deeper, maybe for the lyrics.

All thy faithful mercies crown

I don't look at my brother. It might set us off. I do bump shoulders with him and clear my throat. "Oh, Lord," he says. "No pun intended."

I can't keep myself from laughing, though. I have to hold my nose. Then I realize that if I put my handkerchief to my face and let it come no one will be able to tell the difference between laughter and tears. I feel brilliant.

But in the next moment, and for several after that, I can't tell, either.

After a while Robert puts a hand on my back, and I am instantly quiet. I wonder if I was ever as calming to my father. I only know I meant to be.

I find myself dismayed, not only by Father Marty's cartoonish attempts to get everyone singing hymns they don't know, but also by the absence of beauty, as if my father doesn't deserve it. There are bouquets, refrigerated, arranged by strangers; there is nondescript and inoffensive music playing softly. Maybe this is what my cousin Margaret was feeling earlier: here is the corpse of one we loved; what do we have to put in the other pan of the balance but beauty, however we define it?

I had not planned to eulogize my father. I told myself he would not have wanted it. But now I begin to feel that it's just too easy to snigger about the priest's buffoonishness, smile at my grandson, and patronize my cousin's husband and his morbid photography. I tug at my brother's sleeve. An inescapable charge is suddenly mine: as firstborn son I am required to say something. The mandate is not coming from the room of uncles and aunts and cousins and neighbors sitting in rows of chairs, dabbing at their eyes with folded and refolded tissues, who might have been just as happy to leave it all to the saccharine offices of Father Marty. "I think I'd like to speak," I say to my brother. "I feel like I ought to say something," I add. Joe gives a slight shrug and raises his brows as if to say, "Go ahead, then."

But say what? I rise with the fullness of duty upon me. Duty to whom? To what?

My family and neighbors, my father's friends, seem to flinch slightly when I come forward, and a little breeze of worry, a brief *uh-oh* seems to pass over them. I have a reputation. I am the "yes, but" man. Nobody, in any family, welcomes the "yes, but" person. They may love that person, they may even appreciate his or her candor, but they do not welcome his impudence. For a good while, at least since the local distress caused by my memoir, *Half the House,* died down, I agreed with what I took to be their tolerant judgment: "That's enough out of you now, Dickie. You caused enough trouble."

I'm terrified. I don't know what I'm going to say, not the first word of it. I only know that I will regret it forever if I let the moment pass in silence. I have, somehow, the rusty taste of blood in the back of my throat, so that I wipe my nose on a tissue and glance at it, expecting to see the bright red I can taste there. No. The room is full of expectation, apprehension, here and there some anger: *Here he is, the son who shamed his father, who hung out the family laundry, who complained.* Or so I imagine.

I turn to the casket for a moment, and my father smirks at me. "This oughtta be good," he seems about to say.

It's a familiar interaction. If I'd been caught doing some-thing forbidden, or coming in late, my father would demand an explanation, and during my stammering or throat clear-ing, he'd say, "This oughtta be good," as if expecting me to fabricate an alibi, almost as if not at least making a good effort would have disappointed him.

I blurt, "I loved my father very much," and stop, not sure where I'll take it from there. I can almost hear him behind me. "Oh, for Christ's sake, that's the best you can come up with?"

I went on to improvise for about five or ten minutes, but I can't remember much of what I said. I spoke about games, about fairness, about the sense of justice modeled by games—by fair play, boundaries. I mentioned my father's striped referee's shirt and black leather officiating shoes, his whistle on a lanyard I made him one rainy day at the play-ground. I remember that I said he loved my mother and that his favorite ice cream was butter pecan. That his life was shaped by poverty and war. That he didn't expect life to be fair, only that the rules be the same for everyone. I talked about his caring for my brothers in their illnesses, how hard he took their deaths. I said he was a complicated man. All the while I felt as if one of those Buddhist sky funerals were taking place in my head, in which a deceased monk's body is carried to the top of a mountain by his fellows, who then watch and meditate upon the great feast it provides for the birds of the air; their terrible hooked beaks and screeching appetites were the need I still had to know and understand him, alighting upon his life from this angle and that, pulling and tearing at his now-inanimate history. As I was talking, trying to be coherent, trying to keep it simple, say something true, speaking without knowing what I would say next, and what after that, or if I had already gone on too long, or if there was any way I could bring this to a close, the wheeling birds got louder and louder, and I knew that I would have to write about my father again.

There is one more opportunity to approach the bier before the undertaker closes the casket. Only a few people do. Veronica approaches and kneels there for a moment, crying, and D runs across the open space to her. She sniffs, wipes her eyes, and picks him up, then continues to kneel another moment while he stares, sucking his thumb. Does he, can he, recall the weekend three months before, when they met? Veronica rises and turns, and D twists in her arms to point at his great-grandfather with his wet thumb. He blurts a syllable, a cry, a sound almost a word.

Back at the house, Joe sat down in my father's chair by the window. I sat across from him on the sofa. The TV's vast expanse of olive drab reflected and distorted both of us. "I thought Father Marty was going to take off!" I said.

"Yeah, he looked like he believed that if he flapped his arms enough, we all might fly."

"Nobody knew the words! I felt sorry for him."

"Yeah, right. You weren't laughing at him, you were laughing with him. Gimme a break."

"At least we have a photographic record!"

We both laughed again at Henry's picture taking, shook our heads, and fell silent.

Somewhere in the detritus of this house there is an ironing board, somewhere the glass bottle I sprayed with blue enamel and, after it had dried, painted orange and yellow flowers on it and fitted it with a ceramic sprinkler, a Cub Scout project my mother used forever after when ironing.

Somewhere in a corner of the middle room closet, deep in the dark, is a long-idle vacuum cleaner. On the windowsill above the kitchen sink is a plastic watering pot with a long spout, inside it the powdery residue of the limestone water in that part of Pennsylvania, useless in a house where nothing grows. Pots and pans and baking sheets, a flower sifter, many wooden spoons, unmoved for twenty-five years, beyond their use, as past, as dead as my mother.

Once again I'm steeped in grief, not only for my father, but for my mother and my brothers. The house is filled with the stale air of past mourning. I can hardly breathe. And I am struck, again, by my brother's strong resemblance to our father, sitting there by the window in his chair.

My father rose every morning for twenty-five years, made himself a pot of coffee and a piece of toast, turned on his gigantic television, and sat in that chair. For a man given to extremes of grief and rage, to violent turns of emotion, the safety of that chair, that calm against the many years of crisis, that precarious psychic equilibrium, was no small achievement, and no small reward for years of bitter injustice, profound fatigue, incessant obligation, and acute desperation. Goddamn it, he was going to savor every minute of it. We called it depression; he thought he'd earned the right to do nothing. He seemed to have found a deep and comfortable repose. Stuck in that chair—he could yank on the lever and rock back into his favorite position—he was in fact returning to the difficult balance he'd found, like a spirit level, bubble balanced steady in the middle. Nothing was wrong, so everything must be all right.

I have come to think of it as the injury chair—my grandfather took to it when he was injured and disabled, my father when he had had enough, when the deaths of his sons and his wife had undone him, and even me, in the hand-me-down recliner, nursing a stiff Jim Beam, keeping the rapes and the beatings unremembered. The injury chair.

Recently I discovered that the root meaning of the word injury is "not fair."

The phone rang. Several times. "You want me to get that?" I asked.

"Let the machine answer it."

The next voice was my father's. "You have reached the Hoffmans. No one can come to the phone right now. Please leave a message and we'll call you back." The sound of his voice was no comfort. It was the funeral home, asking my brother to call back.

The funeral director was sorry to report that the grave-diggers refused to dig the grave, that they required more notice.

"The man died on Friday!" Joe shouted into the phone.

The funeral director said she would see what she could do.

"What the hell?" my brother said to me. He looked desperate, as if we had gotten this close to getting our father safely in the ground and now—of course!—everything was going wrong. He looked as if he expected to be blamed for it. Absurdity and outrage and grief collided. It turns out that it's possible to laugh in anger and sorrow, and we did.

"What the hell, do they want you to schedule when you're gonna kick now?" my brother says.

"Maybe we should have told him to hurry the hell up or something."

"Gravediggers are pro-*fesh*-ionals now. You can't just die without an appointment!"

"You can't just drop in!"

I remember that we laughed and laughed, unless that was crying.

&

Burials are a weird business these days. Flaps of carpet cover the walls of the grave itself, and the casket rests on straps on a frame of brass, where it will remain until the last door of the last car with its lights on midday thunks shut, and the procession crunches gravel toward the gate. Levers are released and, just like jacking down a car after fixing a tire, the departed is more or less smoothly lowered to the bottom of the grave.

Even so, standing there on the strip of faux grass, between my son and my brother, I could smell earth. The pile of dirt that had been removed was covered by a tarp. Still, I could smell the earth as fresh as the backyard dirt I played in as a boy; and the scent of late-summer grass, of broken turf. I put a hand on Robert's shoulder as I lean forward to place a red rose on my father's grave, my mother's as well—she under him, my parents' beside my brothers' graves—and I know that I am now but one remove from earth.

No longer the fruit, but the tree.

Acknowledgments

My thanks to Kathleen Aguero, Veronica Aguero-Hoffman, Robert Aguero-Hoffman, Ashley Alexander, Richard Cambridge, Helen Fremont, Joseph Hoffman, Lee Hope, Joe Mackall, William B. Patrick, Frederick Reiken, Michael Steinberg, Mimi Schwartz, Karen Wulf, and Mako Yoshikawa for reading and commenting on portions of this book.

I want to thank Emerson College, particularly president Lee Pelton, for a leave of absence during which the final draft of this book was written.

As always, I am grateful to "the soup group"—Mike, Thom, Ellen, Steve, and Zoya—for their personal support.

Abundant thanks to my editor, Alexis Rizzuto; this is truly her book, too.